Lead Like Jesus
Study Guide

· ·

Lessons from the Greatest
Leadership Role Model of All Time

Ken Blanchard and Phil Hodges

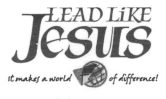

LEAD LiKE JESUS

It makes a world of difference!

LeadLikeJesus.com

Published byThe Center for Faithwalk Leadership dba Lead Like Jesus, 3506 Professional Circle, Augusta, GA 30907; 800.383.6890; LeadLikeJesus.com

Unless otherwise noted, Scripture quotations are taken from the HOLY BIBLE, NEW INTERNATIONAL VERSION®. NIV®. Copyright©1973, 1978, 1984 by International Bible Society. Used by permission of Zondervan. All rights reserved.

Scripture quotations marked PHILLIPS are taken from The New Testament in Modern English, Revised Edition by J.B. Phillips. Copyright J. B. Phillips 1958, 1961, 1972. Used by permission of Macmillan Publishing Company, a division of Macmillan, Inc.

Scripture quotations marked MSG are taken from the The Message, copyright © 1993. Used by permission of NavPress Publishing Group.

Scripture quotations marked KJV are taken from The King James Version of the Bible.

Scripture quotations marked NASB are taken from the New American Standard Bible®, Copyright © 1960, 1962, 1963, 1968, 1971, 1972, 1973, 1975, 1977, 1995 by The Lockman Foundation. Used by permission.

ISBN-13: 978-0-9793855-0-6

ISBN-10: 0-9793855-0-4

Printed in the United States of America.

06 07 08 09 – 9 8 7 6 5 4 3 2 1

table of contents

preface

ARE YOU A LEADER?

Whenever we pose this question to an audience and ask for a show of hands some people respond quickly and others do not raise their hands at all. Why is that?

The reason probably has to do with their personal definition and image of a leader. For many people, the word *leader* calls up the image of someone in an organization with a formal title such as President, Manager, Coach, General, Pastor, Director, or Captain. It rarely includes all of the informal leadership that is going on around them and plays a major role in what they do and think in every aspect of their lives.

Think about the people in your life who have most influenced your thinking, behavior, and life path. If, as with most people, your list includes family members and friends, you will quickly realize that leaders with formal titles and positions of authority only make up part of the leadership landscape.

Leadership is an influence process. Any time you seek to influence the thinking, behavior, or development of another person, you're engaging in a leadership moment.

Leadership can be as intimate as words of guidance and encouragement to a loved one or as impersonal as providing operating instructions to an entire organization.

Each of the people in the following situations is engaged in an act of leadership. All are exerting influence through their choices to either act or refrain from action. Some are exhibiting qualities of servant leadership, while others are being self-serving leaders:

- a parent with a young child at any time of day
- a friend risking an angry response to point out a moral failure
- a local pastor who avoids teaching on controversial issues for fear of rejection
- a business executive rejecting inside information that would give him a competitive edge
- a military commander equipping his troops to go into harm's way
- a middle school teacher who excites curiosity in the minds of her students
- a rehabilitation nurse who patiently handles the anger of a stroke victim
- a high school coach who fails to confront rule violations by his star player
- an adult child providing guidance on living arrangements to an aging parent
- a government official who takes an unpopular political stand based on principle
- a dictator who hoards millions of dollars while his citizens are starving

Each of these leaders is involved in making personal choices about how and to what end they will use their influence. It is the same choice we are all called to make when we exert influence in all of our relationships: *Will we seek to serve or to be served?*

When Jesus spoke to His first disciples about the answer to this question He made it clear beyond any doubt that the answer should always be "to serve." The servant leadership that Jesus taught and modeled was radically different from the self-serving leadership that was being practiced in all aspects of the daily life of His first century disciples. It required them to trust Him to tell them the truth and to guide them on the path that they should go. As His followers today, He is calling us to the same radical approach to leadership that is in sharp contrast to the model the world around us provides. The questions we must decide are: who will we follow and how will we lead?

introduction

Every person who picks up this *Lead like Jesus Study Guide* must answer the same question—Why? Why are you even considering a study guide about leading like Jesus?

Read through the following statements and check those that most nearly reflect your reasons for considering this *Lead Like Jesus Study Guide*?

____ curiosity: as a Christian I never thought of Jesus as leader before

____ somebody made this required reading

____ to consider the option of leading like Jesus to other leadership models

____ to find help in advancing my career by becoming a better leader

____ to discover some new ideas to teach to the men's group at church

____ to get resources for my spouse, who is struggling at work

____ I am so overwhelmed with my role as a leader, I will try anything

____ to be more Christ like in all I do, including the way I lead

____ to learn to apply Christian leadership methods to my business

____ to improve the performance of the people I lead, so that we will reach our common goals and objectives

____ to learn how to resolve conflicts between my spiritual life and my work life

IMPORTANT IF TRUE

Jesus said, "Come to me, all you who are weary and burdened, and I will give you rest. Take my yoke upon you and learn from me, for I am gentle and humble in heart, and you will find rest for your souls. For my yoke is easy and my burden is light" (Matt. 11:28–30).

As in all things, when Jesus teaches us about leadership, He teaches what is both right and what works to bring us into fulfillment of our highest purpose—to glorify God. As we seek to learn how to lead from Him, Jesus promises us the sweetest of gifts, peace for our souls.

Jesus is both the Teacher and the Lesson. He offers an open invitation to all people to come to him and receive the greatest of gifts: salvation for our souls. But in coming to Him we must do so, not by forced obedience but willingly. He accepts any ready servant, no matter how limited the level of service. We don't have to fear His yoke. His commandments are holy, just, and good. It requires self-surrender, and it exposes us to difficulties, but this is abundantly repaid, even in this world, by inward peace and joy. It is a yoke that is lined with love.

So powerful is the help He gives us, so suitable the encouragements, and so strong the consolations to be found in the way of duty, that we may truly learn to say it is a yoke of pleasantness. The way of duty is the way of rest. The truths Christ teaches are such as we may venture our souls upon.[1]

Are you tired of trying to figure things out by yourself? Do you find leadership a joy-stealing burden? Are you ready to accept the invitation of the ultimate leadership Teacher to come just as you are—warts and all—to learn from Him? If your answer is yes, just bow your head for a moment and tell Him in your own words.

OUR HOPE FOR YOU

We want you to experience Jesus in a whole different way—to grow to trust Him as the perfect One to follow as you seek to lead others. This involves surrendering our lives and leadership to Him. The real secret to leading like Jesus is found in Proverbs 3:5–6 : "Trust in the Lord with all your heart and lean not on your own understanding; in all your ways acknowledge him, and he will make your paths straight."

Jesus is clear about how He wants us to lead. He asks us to make a difference in our world by being effective servant leaders. It is our prayer and desire that this *Lead Like Jesus Study Guide* will be the beginning of a new and exciting chapter in your personal journey to becoming just that. It is designed to guide you in exploring your personal response to Jesus's call to "follow Me" and to put into action the principles of servant leadership.

Don't worry if you do not have a formal leadership role. The principles are applicable to your relationship with your spouse, kids, friends, coworkers, colleagues, and casual acquaintances. This isn't the intellectual pursuit of a complicated philosophy of leadership; it is a guide to a more practical application of the truths of Scripture. We want you to think differently, but we also want you to develop a lifestyle that is built upon and governed by your relationship with Jesus Christ—the ultimate leader!

HOW THIS STUDY GUIDE IS DESIGNED

We have designed this guide for daily study so that the principles you learn can be consistently put to work in your daily life. We will work from the inside out—that is, we will begin with your motivations, leadership point of view, behaviors, and habits and then we will work out into your spheres of influence as a leader. As you are challenged to look at your own leadership, resist the temptation to respond in ways that you wish things were but do not actually reflect your current, *up-to-now* motivations, attitudes, actions, and beliefs. The truth of the moment may not be pretty. But Jesus said "the truth will set you free" (John 8:32) and so it will, when you confront it with honesty and the knowledge that, in Jesus, we have received the ultimate expression of God's unconditional love and forgiveness.

Each day's study will consist of the following elements:

- **Quote for Today:** A wise word to get us started in the right direction.

- **What God's Word Says:** We will seek first the kingdom by God by looking to His Word as our source of wisdom and direction. When God's Word speaks specifically of how followers of Jesus are to walk a different path from the world around them in heart, mind, body, and spirit, we will seek not to ask *why*, but rather *how*.

- **Pause and Reflect:** This is an opportunity to consider the proposed concept and to record your reaction to it.

- **A Prayer for Today:** Following in the habit of Jesus, we will make prayer our first response instead of our last resort. As we invite the Holy Spirit to guide our thoughts, we will take time to read the prayer for the day and offer it up to God as our own.

- **Today's Topic:** Segments from *Lead Like Jesus: Lessons from the Greatest Leadership Role Model of all Time*, a book by Ken Blanchard and Phil Hodges on which this study guide is based.

- **Look Inside:** Through the use of a variety of learning tools, questionnaires, and exercises, we will explore our *up-to-now* leadership motivations, thinking, behavior, and habits and how they compare with leading like Jesus.

- **Key Concepts:** As we explore leading like Jesus, we will discover key principles, concepts, and nonnegotiable mandates that we are not able to accomplish on our own but are called to implement under the guidance of the Holy Spirit.

• **A Point to Ponder:** a thought or idea to keep with us throughout the day.

 • **Next Steps:** *Lead Like Jesus* will be a lifetime journey to be traveled in His company step-by-step, moment-by-moment. At the end of each day's lesson, you will be asked to prayerfully consider your next steps.

How Can You Reap the Greatest Benefits from This Study?

1. Pray for insight each day as you meet the Lord through this study. Let Him lead you to experience His direction in your life through every learning activity.

2. Experience the focus for each day as you study and apply it to your life. Write down those *Aha!* ideas that challenge your leadership behaviors and motives. Ask yourself how you can realign your leadership to better reflect Christ's example.

3. Review your progress each week and recognize what God is doing in your life and in the lives of those you lead.

4. Keep a journal in which you will list the action steps and plans associated with your *Aha!* ideas. Additionally, write down specific ways in which you are putting into practice what you are learning.

5. Participate in the group sessions, or meet weekly with a study partner. As your group follows the instructions in the Facilitator's Guide (see page 174 for information to download your Facilitator's Guide from www.LeadLikeJesus.com), your knowledge of the principles and their application to everyday life will be multiplied. You cannot learn to lead like Jesus unless you interact with other people. If a small group study isn't possible, get one or two other people to go through the study with you.

We hope as you learn to trust Jesus as your leadership model, it will make you an active agent for restoring joy to work and family. So whether you're leading in business, nonprofit organizations, your community, your church, or your home, you will make Jesus smile. It is the vision of the Lead Like Jesus ministry (LeadLikeJesus.com) that someday, everywhere, everyone will know someone who is truly leading like Jesus. Join us as we step forward together to come closer to the One who beckons us to follow.

A Point to Ponder

Imagine this setting: You, Jesus, and the authors of this *Study Guide* are sitting together conversing about His kind of leadership. Just as the Master Teacher did with His disciples, you will be asked questions, given assignments, and told stories and examples that will help you connect your own experiences with leading like Jesus. So, as you interact with this study guide, invite the Holy Spirit to guide you to new insights and a new perspective on how to put what you learn into practice. Together we will learn to lead like Jesus!

week one

WHO WILL YOU FOLLOW? HOW WILL YOU LEAD?

Memory Verse for the Week

"Not so with you. Instead, whoever wants to become great among you must be your servant, and whoever wants to be first must be your slave--just as the Son of Man did not come to be served, but to serve, and to give His life as a ransom for many" (Matt. 20:26–28).

Welcome and thanks for joining us on this journey to lead like Jesus. This week we will begin by covering some basic information that will set the foundation for the following weeks, when we will explore the *Heart, Head, Hands,* and *Habits* of Jesus as it relates to leadership.

For followers of Jesus, seeking to lead like Jesus is an expression of the ongoing obedience to the one we call Lord. For non-believers, servant leadership may be one option among many, but for followers of Jesus it is a mandate. Jesus gave no plan B option to His first disciples, or His modern-day ones, for how they were to lead and serve one another. The truly exciting part about following Jesus is that He never sends you into any situation alone or with a faulty plan. As in all things when Jesus speaks to us about leadership He speaks what is both right and effective.

When Jesus tells us to do something it can be done.

Our question should not be Why? but How?

Are you ready to find out? Let's begin!

week one

day one | 1 •

WHAT DOES IT MEAN TO LEAD LIKE JESUS?

Quote for the Day

As followers of Jesus, we can trust Him regardless of our circumstances, and we can freely ask Him to give us wisdom in all things, including our leadership roles.[1]

Ken Blanchard and Phil Hodges

What God's Word Says

"For I know the plans I have for you," declares the Lord, "plans to prosper you and not to harm you, plans to give you hope and a future. Then you will call upon me and come and pray to me, and I will listen to you. You will seek me and find me when you seek me with all your heart. I will be found by you," declares the Lord. . . (Jer. 29:11–14)

Pause and Reflect

What does the passage above say about God's desire to be involved in your life?

_____

_____

_____

_____

_____

_____

 A Prayer for Today

Eternal One who never changes, capture my perspective today and plant in me the truth that You are always the same, that Your words are forever true. As You were relevant when You walked the earth, so You are today. In Jesus's Name, Amen!

Today's Topic
WHAT DOES IT MEAN TO LEAD LIKE JESUS?

The essence, the core concept, of leading like Jesus is encapsulated in the *not so with you* mandate that Jesus gave to His disciples. It addressed how they were to carry out leadership roles among them. In Matthew 20:25–28, we read,

> Jesus called them together and said, "You know that the rulers of the Gentiles lord it over them, and their high officials exercise authority over them. **Not so with you**. Instead, whoever wants to be great among you must be your servant, and whoever wants to be first must be your slave—just as the Son of Man did not come to be served, but to serve, and to give his life as a ransom for many."

This call by Jesus to servant leadership is clear and unequivocal; His words leave no room for plan B. He placed no restrictions or limitations of time, place, or situation that would allow us to exempt ourselves from His command. For followers of Jesus, servant leadership isn't an option, it's a mandate. Servant leadership is to be a living statement of who we are in Christ, how we treat one another, and how we demonstrate the love of Christ to the whole world. If this sounds like serious business with profound implications—it is!

As in all things, when Jesus speaks to us about leadership, He speaks about what is right and effective. We can trust His Word as an expression of His unconditional love and concern for our eternal well-being.

As followers of Jesus, we can trust Him regardless of our circumstances, and we can freely ask Him to give us wisdom in all things, including our leadership roles. James 1:2-8 (PHILLIPS, emphasis added) reminds us that Jesus wants to be intimately involved in all aspects of our lives:

> When all kinds of trials and temptations crowd into your lives, my brothers, *don't resent them as intruders, but welcome them as friends!* Realize that they come to test your faith and to produce in you the quality of endurance. But let the process go on until that endurance is fully developed, and you will find you have become men of mature character with the right sort of independence. And *if, in the process, any of you does not know how to meet any particular problem he has only to ask God—who gives generously to all men without making them feel foolish or guilty—and he may be quite sure that the necessary wisdom will be given him.* But he must ask in sincere faith without secret doubts as to whether he really wants God's help or not. The man who trusts God, but with inward reservations, is like a wave of the sea, carried forward by the wind one moment and driven back the next. That sort of man cannot hope to receive anything from God, and the life of a man of divided loyalty will reveal instability at every turn.

Look Inside

- Review Matthew 20:25–28. What phrase does Jesus use to distinguish between the leadership principles of the Gentiles and His leadership principles?

- How does this call from Jesus to be and act differently relate to His followers today?

_____ Christians are called to obey Jesus's commands only when dealing with other believers. It is fine to adopt the world's ways when dealing with non-believers.

_____ Christians are called to obey Jesus's commands in all relationships, especially relationships with non-believers, because many non-believers get their ideas about God from their interactions with people who claim to be Christians.

_____ Since Jesus said this more than two thousand years ago, in simpler times, it has little relevance to today.

- If Jesus were in your position of leadership at work, how would His leadership style differ from yours? List three responses.

1 _____

_____

2 _____

_____

3 _____

_____

- Think about your other leadership roles—father, mother, church leader, etc. How would Jesus's leadership style differ from your leadership style? List three responses.

1 _____

_____

2 _____

_____

3 _____

_____

- List some reasons you might doubt the effectiveness of Jesus's leadership model.

_____

_____

_____

_____

Key Concepts

- For a follower of Jesus, servant leadership isn't an option, it's a mandate.
- Servant leadership is to be a living statement of who we are in Christ and how we demonstrate the love of Christ to the whole world.
- As in all things, when Jesus speaks to us about leadership, He speaks about what is right and effective.
- We can trust His Word as an expression of His unconditional love and sacrifice for our eternal well-being.
- As followers of Jesus, we can trust Him regardless of our circumstances, and we can freely ask Him to give us wisdom in all things, including our leadership roles.

Point to Ponder

We believe that if you apply what it means to lead like Jesus to your *heart, head, hands,* and *habits,* you will be in a position to radically transform your leadership.

Next Steps

Identify three people that you influence through a one-on-one relationship:

_____

_____

_____

Considering each of your relationships with these three people, fill in the statements below:

In my relationship with _____, I want to demonstrate my desire to be more of a servant leader by taking the following action: _____

_____

In my relationship with _____, I want to demonstrate my desire to be more of a servant leader by taking the following action: _____

_____

In my relationship with _____, I want to demonstrate my desire to be more of a servant leader by taking the following action: _____

_____

week one

day two | **2** • •

WOULD YOU HIRE JESUS AS YOUR LEADERSHIP COACH AND GUIDE?

Quote for the Day

Jesus understood from years of personal experience the challenges of daily life and work. Although Jesus was God, He was not ashamed to do a man's work.[2]

Ken Blanchard and Phil Hodges

What God's Word Says

Now that we know what we have—Jesus, this great High Priest with ready access to God—let's not let it slip through our fingers. We don't have a priest who is out of touch with our reality. He's been through weakness and testing, experienced it all—all but the sin. (Heb. 4:14–15 MSG)

Pause and Reflect

The passage above reveals something about God's desire to be involved in guiding your life. Reflect on the passage and then write a short note to God expressing your acceptance or rejection of His involvement in your life. Explain your response.

_____

_____

_____

_____

A Prayer for Today

Never-changing Lord whose love and compassion are new every morning, help me to know and live in the truth that You are the Source and the Teacher of all wisdom. Help me to live and lead in a way that glorifies Your name. In Jesus's Name, Amen!

Today's Topic
WOULD YOU HIRE JESUS AS YOUR LEADERSHIP COACH AND GUIDE?

A common barrier to embracing Jesus as a leadership role model lies in skepticism about the relevance of His teaching to your specific leadership situations. One way of putting Jesus to the test would be to apply the same criteria to His knowledge, experience, and success that you would to the hiring of a leadership consultant or coach.

If you were looking for a coach to advise you in running your day-to-day life, what criteria would you seek? Rank the following criteria in order of preference:

___ Familiarity with the rules of the game

___ Wisdom

___ Knowledge

___ Successful track record

___ Problem-solving

___ Interpersonal skills

___ Personal integrity

___ Ability to diagnose root causes

So, based on His leadership resume would you hire Jesus as a coach?

___ Yes ___ No

If you are inclined to answer *no* take a few moments to reflect on the leadership challenges you might be facing and consider again whether you would hire Jesus as your personal leadership coach based on His experience as a leader.

Jesus was an experienced leader. Consider His qualifications:

- accomplishing a mission with imperfect people
- ability to establish and communicate clear purpose and direction
- recruitment of people to accomplish the task
- training, development, and delegation issues
- conflict management
- managing demands of time, energy, and resources
- dealing with competition
- turnover, betrayal, and lack of understanding by family members
- constant scrutiny and challenges to commitment and integrity
- temptations to misuse power
- handling of criticism, rejection, distractions, and opposition
- personal sacrifice in serving the greatest good

Chances are you said *yes* to every situation. Why? Because Jesus had experience in every situation listed. Since He already has encountered these situations, you can trust the wisdom of His experience. If you were inclined to answer *no* to adopting Jesus as your leadership coach, take a few moments to consider what it is about Jesus, yourself, or your circumstances that make this a hard concept to accept.

_____

_____

_____

_____

 ## Look Inside

List, for your own consideration, your concerns about adopting Jesus as your leadership guide and role model.

A concern about Jesus

_____

_____

A concern about me

_____

_____

A concern about my leadership circumstances

_____

_____

As we proceed together to consider what leading like Jesus means, keep your reservations in mind and continue to test them against what we discover about Jesus, ourselves, and His provisions and purposes for our lives and leadership.

Key Concepts

- Jesus wants to work in and through you and your leadership to accomplish His ultimate purpose: *to glorify God*. As the following Scriptures indicate, Jesus is calling you to be transformed by choosing to trust in His promises.

  "Come, follow Me," Jesus said, "and I will make you fishers of men" (Matt. 4:19).

  "Come to Me, all you who are weary and burdened, and I will give you rest. Take My yoke upon you and learn from Me, for I am gentle and humble in heart, and you will find rest for your souls" (Matt. 11:28–29).

"I am the vine; you are the branches. If a man remains in me and I in him, he will bear much fruit; apart from me you can do nothing" (John 15:5).

"If you love me, you will obey what I command. And I will ask the Father, and he will give you another Counselor to be with you forever—the Spirit of truth. . . " (John 14:15–17).

A Point to Ponder

Coaching is the most important servant-leadership element in helping people to accomplish their goals.

▶ Next Steps

What are three ways in which you can personally seek to engage Jesus as the source of guidance in your daily decisions? List them below:

1 _____
_____

2 _____
_____

3 _____
_____

How can these decisions from above impact your relationships with the three people you listed in yesterday's Next Steps on page 13?

_____
_____
_____
_____
_____
_____
_____
_____
_____
_____
_____
_____

week one
day three | **3** ● ● ●

LEADING LIKE JESUS IS A TRANSFORMATIONAL JOURNEY, PART 1

Quote for Today

Learning to lead like Jesus is more than an announcement; it is a commitment to lead in a different way. This change will not happen overnight . . . leading like Jesus is a transformational cycle that begins with personal leadership and then moves to leading others in one-on-one relationships, then to leading a team or group, and finally, to leading an organization or community.[3]

Ken Blanchard and Phil Hodges

What God's Word Says

If you love me, you will obey what I command. And I will ask the Father, and he will give you another Counselor to be with you forever—the Spirit of truth. The world cannot accept him, because it neither sees him nor knows him. But you know him, for he lives with you and will be in you. I will not leave you as orphans; I will come to you. (John 14:15–18)

Pause and Reflect

The Scripture above features an "if-then" statement. What is the end result ("then" statement) that we are seeking?

_____

Under what conditions will that desire be met? (See the "if" statement.)

_____

_____

What causes you more difficulty—living up to Jesus's conditions or accepting the guidance of the Holy Spirit? Explain your response.

_____

_____

A Prayer for Today

Lover of all mankind and Lover of my soul, I want to lead like You. Help me to learn, first of all, to be like You so that from the overflow of my grateful heart others will see You in my leadership. In Jesus's Name, Amen!

Today's Topic

LEADING LIKE JESUS IS A TRANSFORMATIONAL JOURNEY, PART 1

The diagram below shows that leading like Jesus is a transformational journey. It begins with personal leadership, then moves to leadership in one-on-one relationships, then leadership in teams or family, and finally, leadership in organizations or communities. We feel this sequence holds up whether you are talking about life role leadership, which occurs in enduring relationships such as those of parent, spouse, sibling, friend, and citizen, or organizational leadership.

Transformational Leadership Model

Personal Leadership
Outcome = Perspective
Matthew 3:13–4:11

Organizational/Community Leadership
Outcome = Effectiveness/Reconciliation
Matthew 28:19–20

One-on-One Leadership
Outcome = Trust
Matthew 4:18–24

Team/Family Leadership
Outcome = Community/Legacy
Matthew 10:5–10

Personal Leadership

Effective leadership starts on the inside. Before you can hope to lead anyone else as Jesus would, you have to know yourself. Every leader must answer two critical questions: *Whose am I?* and *Who am I?*

The first question, Whose am I?, deals with choosing the primary authority and audience for your life. In other words, whom are you trying to please? Leaders often demonstrate whose they are in how they define success in today's world. They think success has to do with earthly power and position, as well as performance and the opinions of others.

You can state it any way you like, but Scripture teaches us that ultimately we are created to please God.

In the Personal Leadership arena, the first choice you will make is whether or not you will seek to *please God first as your leadership priority*. Jesus called us to this purpose when He said, "Seek ye first the Kingdom of God" (Matt. 6:33 KJV).

The question, Who am I?, deals with your life purpose. Why did the Lord put you on earth? What does He want to do through you? Scripture teaches that true success is the fulfillment of the life mission God planned for you. The natural outcome of deciding to please God is to change your *perspective* about what is of greatest importance from God's point of view. If you live a life not committed to pleasing God first or giving Him control, your perspective will be focused inward and on self. It will be from that self-dominated perspective that your motivations in leading others will flow.

As He stepped forward at the beginning of His season of leadership, Jesus demonstrated His commitment and submission to please only the Father when He urged John to baptize Him "to fulfill all righteousness" (Matt. 3:15). He then went into the wilderness and was tempted by Satan. In resisting the temptations of instant gratification, recognition, and misuse of power, Jesus affirmed Whose He was and Who He was. In all these situations, Jesus chose the will of His Father.

Look Inside

Check the choices below that represent your honest response to the question, "Up to now, whom have you been trying to please most?"

_____ your boss	_____ your coworkers	_____ your neighbors
_____ your spouse	_____ your friends	_____ your parents
_____ your children	_____ God	_____ yourself

Developing Your Own Personal Lead-Like-Jesus Perspective

After thinking and teaching about leading like Jesus for several years, Phil Hodges began to feel personally disconnected from the message he was preaching. One afternoon, before presenting a Lead Like Jesus Encounter (see page 173), Phil sat quietly in his hotel room, striving to reconnect with what the message of Lead Like Jesus meant to him personally. In this time of reflection, Phil wrote the following statements.

1. I have been called and have accepted the invitation to enter into a special personal relationship with Jesus Christ as my Savior, my Lord, my teacher, and my friend.

2. As a follower of Jesus, I enjoy the great privilege of personal access to His wisdom and His provisions for living in harmony with His plan for me, a spiritual being with an eternal destiny in God's great universe.

3. I am the object of God's affection, and through the blood of Jesus I enjoy an inexhaustible supply of unconditional love, acceptance, and value that is not dependent on my performance.

4. I am the temporary steward of a wide variety of riches on loan from God to be enjoyed, maintained, and used only for their intended purpose.

5. I will be called to give account for my stewardship when all the things of this world are returned to their owner.

6. All those I seek to lead are made in God's image and are the objects of His affection. He calls me to treat them as His special concern.

7. By seeking to serve rather than be served as I lead others, I will make Jesus smile.

8. Jesus never calls me to follow a flawed plan or a plan to fail, including how I am to lead others.

9. I have been called not to success, but to obedience as a witness to others and as an active agent of God's plan for His kingdom.

10. I accept and find joy in the truth that apart from Jesus I can do nothing alone, but I can do all things through Christ who strengthens me.

Re-read each of the perspectives statements and place a check mark [✔] by the statements that most closely reflect your own *up-to-now* perspective and an *X* by the statements that seem furthest from your *up-to-now* perspective.

Consider the statements you marked with an *X*. Which of the following words describes your reasons for resistance to God? Write the words in the margin beside each statement:

Fear

Doubt

Pride

Unbelief

Past

Experiences

Other: _____.

As we proceed on our journey, we will return to these common barriers and observe their impact on the effectiveness of leadership.

 ## Key Concepts

- Effective leadership starts in the heart of the leader.
- Before you can hope to lead anyone else as Jesus would, you have to decide if pleasing God first will be your personal priority.
- The natural outcome of deciding to please God, as well as deciding to turn over control of your life to Him, is to change your *perspective* to one focused on glorifying Him by carrying His love and grace into all your relationships.
- There are powerful barriers that can prevent us from leading like Jesus, and they can only be overcome by faith in the promises of God.

 ## A Point to Ponder

When Jesus called His disciples to follow Him, His promise was to *make them fishers of men*. He knew they could never make the transformational journey on their own, and He never asked or wanted them to try.

▶ Next Steps

In very simple terms, describe a leader in the space provided.

_____

_____

_____

_____

Now, describe how adding the term *servant* to your answer would change that definition.

_____

_____

_____

_____

_____

_____

TRANSFORMATIONAL JOURNEY, PART 2

Quote for Today

Trust is a stream with a fragile ecological balance: once it is polluted, it will take time and effort to restore.[4]

Ken Blanchard and Phil Hodges

What God's Word Says

But God demonstrates his own love for us in this: While we were still sinners, Christ died for us. (Rom. 5:8)

Pause and Reflect

• When did God's love for you begin?

_____

_____

_____

_____

• At what point should you begin to express love to others?

_____ now!

_____ when they accept Jesus

_____ when they are perfect like me!

_____ never, I'm the only person who matters

A Prayer for Today

Because You are the only One who loves unconditionally and without reservation, Lord, I am amazed. Teach me to love others as You love me, and may I restore and rescue damaged relationships and broken trusts through the power of Your love flowing through me. In Jesus's Name, Amen!

Today's Topic
LEADING LIKE JESUS TRANSFORMATIONAL JOURNEY, PART 2

The first test of the desire to lead like Jesus will come in the arena of one-on-one relationships. The vital outcome will be the level of trust that grows between you and those most directly impacted by you. Without *trust* it is impossible for any relationship to reach its highest potential. Trust in a leader is never achieved or maintained if a leader has a self-serving perspective on life. People will never move toward him or her. We can turn to Jesus again as our example.

At the beginning of His ministry, after spending time in the wilderness, where he affirmed that pleasing His Father was His highest priority, Jesus began the process of calling His disciples. Once they agreed to follow Him, Jesus spent three years building a culture of trust between Himself and these men.

In life role relationships, trust is the stream on which vulnerability, caring, commitment, and grace flow between parents and children, husbands and wives, brothers and sisters, friends and fellow citizens. Trust pours first from loving hearts committed to serve and support one another, through promises kept to encouragement and appreciation expressed, through support and acceptance to repentance and apologies accepted, reconciliation, and restoration. Yet trust is a stream with a fragile ecological balance. Once it is polluted, it will take time and effort to restore.

The always-present power to restore intimacy and broken trust is love. Read the following words from the apostle Paul, and ponder anew the cleansing and healing properties of love:

Love is patient, love is kind. It does not envy, it does not boast, it is not proud. It is not rude, it is not self-seeking, it is not easily angered, it keeps no record of wrongs. Love does not delight in evil but rejoices with the truth. It always protects, always trusts, always hopes, always perseveres. (1 Cor 13:4–7)

Look Inside

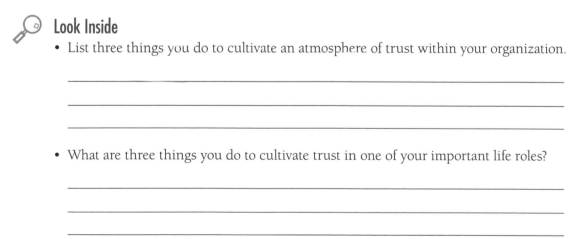

• List three things you do to cultivate an atmosphere of trust within your organization.

_____

_____

_____

• What are three things you do to cultivate trust in one of your important life roles?

_____

_____

_____

- What are two things you do that jeopardize trust within your organization?

  _____

  _____

- What are two things you do to jeopardize trust within your life role?

  _____

  _____

- Think of a time when you lost trust in a leader. What three words best describe how you felt at the time?

  _____

- How long did those feelings affect your relationship with the leader in question?

  _____

- When did you forgive him or her?

  _____ Immediately

  _____ Later

  _____ Never

- How might Jesus have responded in a similar situation?

  _____

  _____

Key Concepts
- Without *trust* it is impossible for any relationship to reach it's highest potential
- Trust is a stream with a fragile ecological balance. Once it is polluted, it will take time and effort to restore.
- The always-present power to restore intimacy and broken trust is love.

A Point to Ponder
It is impossible to go through life without trust: that is to be imprisoned in the worst cell of all, oneself.[5]

Graham Greene

Next Steps
"Therefore, if you are offering your gift at the altar and there remember that your brother has something against you, leave your gift there in front of the altar. First go and be reconciled to your brother; then come and offer your gift." (Matt 5:23-24 NIV)

Consider a person with whom you have a broken trust relationship. Below, write a prayer, asking God to open your heart towards restoration and about what steps you need to take to begin the process of restoring your relationship with that person.

_____

_____

_____

_____

_____

_____

_____

_____

_____

_____

_____

_____

TRANSFORMATIONAL JOURNEY, PART 3

Quote for Today

Effective leaders working at the team level realize that to be good stewards of the energy and efforts of those committed to work with them, they must honor the power of diversity and acknowledge the power of teamwork. As the saying goes, "None of us is as smart as all of us."[6]

Ken Blanchard and Phil Hodges

The rewards of family leadership are most apt to be found in the subtle fashioning of loving relationships and the slow growth of personal character.[7]

Ken Blanchard and Phil Hodges

God's Word Says

Love is patient, love is kind. It does not envy, it does not boast, it is not proud. It is not rude, it is not self-seeking, it is not easily angered, it keeps no record of wrongs. Love does not delight in evil but rejoices with the truth. It always protects, always trusts, always hopes, always perseveres. (1 Cor. 13:4–7)

Pause and Reflect

Read the passage above and rate your love based on the following characteristics.

	This is me!	I have work to do!
I am patient.		
I am kind.		
I do not envy others.		
I never boast.		
I am not prideful.		
I am not rude to others.		
I don't demand my own way.		

	This is me!	I have work to do!
I do not have a problem with anger.		
I don't keep track of what others do to me.		
I delight in what is good.		
I protect, trust, hope, and persevere.		

A Prayer for Today

Loving Father, You are my only hope for loving others. Teach me, as I experience Your love daily, to offer that same love to those I love and lead. In Jesus's Loving Name, Amen!

Today's Topic
LEADING LIKE JESUS TRANSFORMATIONAL JOURNEY, PART 3

Team Leadership

As leaders develop a trusting relationship with people in the one-on-one leadership arena, they become trustworthy. Then they are ready for team development through empowerment. Effective leaders working at the team level realize that to be good stewards of the energy and efforts of those committed to work with them; they must honor the power of diversity and acknowledge the power of teamwork. As the saying goes, "None of us is as smart as all of us."

Once again, we look to Jesus as a model for team leadership. After Jesus spent time personally teaching and modeling the type of leadership He wanted them to adopt, He sent out His disciples to minister in teams of two (Mark 6:7). In doing so, Jesus empowered them to act on His behalf to support one another in accomplishing the work they had been trained to do.

Trust is also a key factor in successful implementation at the team level. Without the trust developed in the one-on-one relationship, empowerment will never happen. Individuals in the group will not empower each other to accomplish an assigned task if they do not trust each other. Failure to empower is one of the key reasons that teams are ineffective.

Family Leadership

When it comes to team leadership in the family, things really get interesting. In family leadership, the leader's efforts and aspirations to serve the best interests of others often come in direct conflict with his or her own immediate priorities and demands. The rewards of family leadership are most apt to be found in the subtle fashioning of loving relationships and the slow growth of personal character. The family leader's example determines how family members treat people of all ages and conditions; how they view success, failure, and adversity; how they solve problems; and how they communicate love and self-worth. If a family leader believes that his self-worth is the result of his performance plus the opinion of others, he is likely to pass on those priorities and values to the next generation by how he treats them. On the other hand, if the family leader demonstrates humility, grace, and an open reliance on God, His Word, and His promises, these traits are likely to flow into the family members.

Sorting out in a family what needs to be done, by whom, by when, and for what purpose can be as challenging as any team leadership situation. In family leadership, the language of love will be taxed to express encouragement in the face of well-meaning yet colossal failures and messes; patience in times of lost focus, lost keys, and lost phone messages; clear direction and purpose to the reluctant, the annoyed, and the clueless; manners and standards to the rebellious and the doubting; and sympathy and grace to the prodigal and wounded.

The outcome of family leadership is more than the income. The family leader passes on his or her values, priorities, heritage, and identity through behaviors that allow interdependence and loyalty. Family leadership is expressed by the development of each member throughout the cycle of life. It is also where external circumstances have the least credibility as an indicator of success.

Coming from circumstances of privilege and opportunity does not guarantee success as God defines it, nor does being raised in circumstances of abuse and poverty consign someone to failure. In any circumstance, at any time, anyone can choose to follow Jesus. In that moment, the external circumstances pale in comparison to the inner resources that knowing and following Jesus provides.

A word of warning: because our life role relationships are based on loyalty and commitment for a lifetime, we can fall into the trap of relying too much on their resilience and our ability to regain lost ground, lost intimacy, and lost love. Life role relationships are worthy of daily renewal and nurture in light of the fact that we never know when and how they will end. As Ken's wife, Margie, often says, "We need to keep our 'I love you's' up to date."

Organizational or Community Leadership

Whether a leader can function well in the organizational leadership arena depends on the outcome of perspective, trust, and community attained at the first three levels in his or her transformational leadership journey. The outcome of focusing on this level is organizational *effectiveness,* both high performance and high human satisfaction. It is important to note that when Jesus began His ministry on earth, He did not start at the organizational level. He could have come to the existing organizations of the faithful in His day and said, "Okay, gentlemen, I'm here, I'm in charge, and this is the way we will change things!" Instead, Jesus chose to take the approach of a servant leader and quietly influence the lives of a small group of men whom He then trusted and empowered to impact the world. By valuing both relationships and results, Jesus created the environment for developing an effective organization.

In His own life, He was aligned with the purpose His Father had for Him. Jesus also clearly identified the purposes for His followers and their organizations when He gave us the Great Commandment and the Great Commission. But Jesus, in His incarnate form, never implemented the organizational level. He equipped His disciples in the first three levels and then sent the Holy Spirit to guide them at the organizational leadership level, a process that we see developing in the book of Acts. When organizational leadership enters into the arena of community leadership, it calls for the leader to willingly extend service for the common good. Life role leadership in the community focuses on finding common ground and reconciliation with people of diverse opinions, backgrounds, priorities, and spiritual perspectives. Community leadership requires love to be spoken in truth and courage with good will and tolerance without wandering from moral and ethical conviction. Jesus spent significant time interacting in positive ways with people who disagreed with Him. He did not isolate Himself from those who disagreed; He embraced those who disagreed. He did not change His message to gain approval, but He continued to love those who did not accept His message.

Community leadership is not restricted or defined by a formal position. It is the willingness to speak out for your values in a manner that recognizes the rights of others and the obligation to honor God in all you do. It means walking the extra mile, turning the other cheek, loving your neighbor, forgiving those who persecute you, and being salt and light.

The various how-to's of leadership in the community include informed, principle-based voting, standing up for what is right over what works, responding with honor when called to serve on juries, praying for all who stand in harm's way on behalf of the community, lending a helping hand to those in need, and seeking to understand those who are different from you. The consequences of community leadership may come as a test of conviction when challenged or attacked. They may come as a temptation to compromise principle for practicality. They may come in the form of recognition that tempts pride. They call for the leader to answer the questions "Who am I?" and "Whose am I?" again and again and again.

The Four Domains of Leading Like Jesus

Leading like Jesus involves the alignment of four leadership domains: *heart, head, hands,* and *habits.* The internal domains—the motivations of your *heart* and the leadership perspective of your *head*—are things you keep inside or even disguise if it suits your purpose. The external domains—your public leadership behavior, or *hands,* and your *habit*s as experienced by others—will determine whether people will follow you.

When your *heart, head, hands,* and *habits* are aligned, extraordinary levels of loyalty, trust, and productivity will result. When these areas are out of alignment, you will experience frustration, mistrust, and diminished long-term productivity.

Heart

Leadership is first a spiritual matter of the *heart.* Whenever you have an opportunity or responsibility to influence the thinking and the behavior of others, the first choice you are called to make is whether to be motivated by self-interest or by the benefit of those you are leading. The *heart* question that Jesus asks is, "Are you a servant leader or a self-serving leader?"

Head

The journey to leading like Jesus starts in the *heart* with motivation. Your intent then travels through another internal domain, the *head,* which examines your beliefs and theories about leading and motivating people. All great leaders have a specific leadership point of view that defines how they see their role and their relationships to those they seek to influence. Throughout His season of earthly leadership, Jesus continued to teach and emphasize His point of view, which was servant leadership. As Jesus said in Mark 10:45, "For even I, the Son of Man, came here not to be served but to serve others, and to give my life as a ransom for many" (NLT).

Hands

Others will experience and observe what is in your *heart* and *head* when your motivations and beliefs about leadership affect your actions (*hands*). If you have a servant heart and a servant leadership point of view, you will become a performance coach. That involves setting clear goals and then observing performance, followed by praising progress and redirecting inappropriate behavior.

Jesus poured Himself into His disciples for three years, so that when He left His earthly ministry they would be able to carry on His vision. The principles of establishing clear goals and measuring performance are common concepts for all types of organizations and apply with equal power to life role leadership relationships.

Habits

Your *habits* are how you renew your daily commitment as a leader to serve rather than to be served. As a leader committed to serve despite all the pressures, trials, and temptations He faced, how did Jesus replenish His energy and servant perspective? His habits! Through a life pattern of solitude and prayer, knowledge of the will of God expressed in His holy Word, and the community He shared with a small group of intimate companions, Jesus was constantly refreshed and renewed.

Are You Willing to Lead Like Jesus?

We believe that if you understand that leading like Jesus is a transformational journey, and if you apply what it means to lead like Jesus to your *heart, head, hands,* and *habits,* you will be in a position to radically transform your leadership. We are confident in this claim, not because of any brilliance on our part but because of the One you will encounter—Jesus.

As you come to know Him in a new way—as the ultimate teacher and model of effective leadership—we hope you will choose to answer His call to "Come, follow me" and learn to lead like Jesus. Are you willing? If not, pass this study guide on to someone else. If you want to lead like Jesus, this study guide will help you discover the leader you already are and the one you can become by learning to lead with your *heart, head, hands,* and *habits* like the greatest leadership role model of all time—Jesus of Nazareth.

Look Inside

- Take a look at the different categories of family leadership actions below and rate yourself from 1 (not doing so well) to 5 (this is my strong point).

    1. Modeling spiritual growth

    1 | 2 | 3 | 4 | 5

    2. Fostering positive personal relationships

    1 | 2 | 3 | 4 | 5

    3. Building others up

    1 | 2 | 3 | 4 | 5

    4. Managing your temper

    1 | 2 | 3 | 4 | 5

    5. Yielding to the needs of others

    1 | 2 | 3 | 4 | 5

    6. Sharing your values

    1 | 2 | 3 | 4 | 5

    7. Godly discipline

    1 | 2 | 3 | 4 | 5

- Look back at the list and note any areas in which you rated yourself a 1 or 2. In the space provided below, list three things you can do to improve your leadership in these areas.

    I can improve _____ by _____

    I can improve _____ by _____

    I can improve _____ by _____

- What words do you think the people in your family would use to describe your leadership in the following situations?

    - In a time of crisis: _____
    - In a time of failure: _____
    - In a time of victory: _____
    - In a time of plenty: _____
    - In a time of want: _____

- Do you like what you think you would hear?_____

If the answer is yes, what aspects of your personal leadership perspective do you believe are at the center of your leadership effectiveness?

_____

_____

_____

_____

If the answer is no, what do you think are the core causes for these negative responses to your leadership?

_____

_____

_____

- What is most likely to occur when leaders try to drive change at the organizational level without first addressing the issue of their own credibility at the personal, one-on-one, and team leadership levels?

_____

_____

_____

 Key Concepts

- Learning to lead like Jesus is more than an announcement; it is a commitment to lead in a different way. It is a transformational cycle that begins with a personal leadership, then moves to leading others in one-on-one relationships, then to leading a team or family, and finally, to leading an organization or community.

- Because our life role relationships are based on loyalty and commitment for a lifetime, we can fall into the trap of relying too much on their resilience and our ability to regain lost ground, lost intimacy, and lost love. Life role relationships are worthy of daily renewal and nurture in light of the fact that we never know when and how they will end.

- Leading like Jesus involves the alignment of four leadership domains: *heart, head, hands,* and *habits.* The internal domains—the motivations of *heart* and the leadership perspective of your *head*—are things you keep inside or even disguise if it suits your purpose. The external domains—your public leadership behavior, or *hands*, and your *habits* as experienced by others—will determine whether people will follow you.

As a conclusion to this week's study we want you to evaluate yourself in preparation for learning to lead like Jesus. Write your answers. This will take time for you to think through them but it will be worth the effort. You will be given the opportunity to share some of your answers in the small group if you desire.

- Up to now, my greatest personal leadership challenge has been:

_____

_____

- Write a brief summary of the greatest recurring challenge you have experienced as a leader in either an organizational setting or in a life role leadership relationship. Describe both your internal struggles and those created by specific relationships and situations.

_____

_____

- Up to now, my reason for assuming the role of a leader has been:

_____

_____

- Up to now, I have measured the success of my organizational leadership efforts based on the following results:

As a Direct Supervisor by _____

As a Team or Group Leader by _____

As a Manager by_____

As a Colleague and Team Member by _____

As an Elder or Governing Board Member by _____

- Up to now, I measured the success of my life role leadership based on following results:

As a parent by _____

As a spouse by _____

As a sibling by _____

As a neighbor by _____

As a friend by _____

As a citizen by _____

- My Leadership Security:

On what do I rely to keep me secure as a leader? (Check all that apply.)

_____ Keeping control	_____ Money
_____ Relationships	_____ Fear
_____ Attention to detail	_____ Performance
_____ Policies	_____ Knowledge
_____ Favors	_____ Busyness
_____ Energy	_____ other: _____
_____ Skill	

- Which of these factors can I trust 100 percent to keep my leadership secure forever?

(Of course, none of these factors will keep you safe forever. Your ultimate security is not found in such behaviors. We will address security in next week's study.)

_____

_____

- What is the focus of your leadership?.

    _____ relationships

    _____ results

    _____ neither

    _____ both

A Point to Ponder

We have covered a lot of territory this week. Don't worry about remembering everything. Throughout this study, we will take time to explore in more depth each aspect of the four dimensions of leadership.

- Briefly summarize one thing God taught you through this week's study.

_____

_____

Pray for your group meeting this week and be prepared to discuss your insights with the other members of your group.

Next Steps

During this week, you've learned about the four domains of leadership. List below the four domains of leadership we've learned about this week, along with one thing you remember about each domain.

_____

_____

_____

_____

_____

_____

_____

_____

_____

_____

week two 2

THE *HEART* OF A SERVANT LEADER

Ours is a love relationship with our heavenly Father. It is grounded in His unconditional love for us as expressed through His Son. It is one in which we are called to love one another—our neighbors and our enemies. Leading like Jesus is an expression of a daily commitment to live out the Word and will of God and thereby advance the kingdom of God. When Jesus was asked what the greatest commandment was, He replied, "Love the Lord your God with all your heart and with all your soul and with all your mind. This is the first and greatest commandment. And the second is like it: 'love your neighbor as yourself'" (Matt. 22:37–39).

Learning to lead like Jesus is, at its essence, learning to love like Jesus.

There are few people who will argue with the fact that our world is in desperate need of leaders. Millions of dollars are spent each year to train people in leadership skills, but there still seems to be a shortage of authentic, ethical leaders. Why? Because most leadership training tries to change leaders from the outside! Most books and seminars focus on leadership behavior and try to improve leadership styles and methods.

In teaching people to lead like Jesus, we have found that effective leadership starts on the inside—it is a heart issue. We believe if you don't get the heart right, then nothing can be done to make you into a servant leader like Jesus.

The problem is the person in the mirror—we came into this world with self-serving hearts. Is there anyone more self-serving than a baby? A baby doesn't come home from the hospital saying, "Can I help you do some things around the house?" The *Lead Like Jesus* journey begins with the transformation from a self-serving heart to a servant heart. You finally become a mature adult when you realize that life is about what you *give* rather than what you *get*. This week we examine what hinders us in moving through this heart journey. We'll take a look at why aligning our hearts with God's plan is a daily battle.

week two

day one | 1 •

2

SELF-SERVING LEADERS VS. SERVANT LEADERS

Quote of the Day

If you want to become the greatest in your field, no matter what it may be, equip yourself to render greater service than anyone else.[1]

Clinton Davidson

What God's Word Says

I will give you a new heart and put a new spirit in you; I will remove from you your heart of stone and give you a heart of flesh. And I will put my Spirit in you and move you to follow my decrees and be careful to keep my laws. (Ezek. 36:26–27)

Pause and Reflect

According to the passage above, God performs surgery on those seeking to follow Him. How is this "surgery" evidenced in your leadership style? Do you reflect the newness that accompanies salvation? Why or why not?

_____

_____

_____

_____

_____

_____

A Prayer for Today

Lord, the only way I can possibly serve others effectively and with meaning is if You give me a new heart. Thanks for that possibility through Jesus! May my new heart be a clear expression of Your love, mercy, and grace. In Jesus's Name, Amen!

Today's Topic

SELF-SERVING LEADERS VS. SERVANT LEADERS

Few people admit to themselves or to others that they are self-serving leaders, yet we see self-serving leaders all the time. We read about them in the paper. We see them going to trial for corporate corruption. We meet them in church work and other volunteer organizations. We experience them in our own families and some times we see them in the mirror.

Self serving leaders operate out of pride and fear, and in turn they drive people by fear or greed, or sometimes encourage others to sacrifice for causes and principles in order to fulfill their own ambitions.

The fact of the matter is that if the stick is big enough, the carrot sweet enough, or the appeal lofty enough, self-serving leaders get results in the short term. The trouble lies in the long term. The impact on the spiritual well-being of both the leaders and the people they influence.

What makes people so self-serving? In his classic book, *Ordering Your Private World,* Gordon McDonald identifies a helpful distinction; he says there are two types of people in the world—*driven* people and *called* people.

Driven people think they own everything. They own their relationships, they own their possessions, they own their positions. In fact, they perceive their identities as the sum total of those relationships, possessions, and positions. As a result they spend most of their time protecting what they own. Driven people believe that "he who dies with the most toys wins." Their possessions are an important part of who they are. We see this type of person in a leadership position where the employees live in constant fear of the leader or the organization.

Called people believe everything they "have" is on loan. Called people believe their possessions, their positions, and their relationships are on loan. Rather than protecting what they own, called leaders believe they need to be good stewards of what has been "loaned" to them.

- What are the differences between driven and called people?

_____

_____

_____

_____

_____

Look Inside

This week we will give you some tests to determine whether you are more of a self-serving leader or a servant leader. We will look at the first two tests today.

Test 1: *Feedback*

Do you welcome and want feedback? Self-serving leaders spend most of their time protecting their status. If you give them feedback—information on how they are doing as a leader—they usually react negatively. They think your feedback means you don't want them to lead anymore. That is their worst nightmare. The biggest fear self-serving leaders have is losing their positions, because much of their self-image is tied up in their positions.

- How do you usually respond to positive feedback?

React negatively – React positively

        1   2   3   4   5

- How do you usually respond to negative feedback?

React negatively – React positively

        1   2   3   4   5

- Explain any difference between the way you respond to positive and negative feedback.

_____

_____

Test 2: *Succession Planning*

Are you preparing a successor for when your season of leadership is complete? In Matthew 25:21, Jesus summed up what we all would like to hear when final judgment is rendered for our efforts to make a difference—"Well done, good and faithful servant!" One aspect of a job well done as a servant leader is how you prepare others to carry on after your season of leadership is completed. Perhaps you haven't thought of your leadership position as a *season* of leadership. But if you reflect on your experience, you probably can see that you have had several seasons of leadership as you have been promoted from one position to another or volunteered for different projects in your community. In the family your succession-planning efforts are centered around preparing your children to effectively manage their own lives. Remember all your leadership positions are on loan to you.

- Check all the ways that you are preparing others to succeed you in your present season of leadership:

_____ modeling what they are to do

_____ consciously teaching them to do your job after you are gone

_____ talking to them about assuming your position

_____ sharing your *trade secrets* so they will be successful

_____ delegating work to them and then giving them helpful feedback

_____ giving them special projects to develop them as leaders

_____ recommending them to superiors

_____ developing a succession plan and keeping a file on possible successors

_____ constantly helping them move from dependence to independence

Servant leaders look beyond their own season of leadership and help to prepare the next generation of leaders. In the use of His time and efforts on earth, Jesus modeled a sacrificial passion for ensuring that His followers were equipped to carry on the movement. He lived His legacy in intimate relationship with those He empowered by His words and example.

Jesus said, "I no longer call you servants, because a servant does not know his master's business. Instead I call you friends, for everything that I learned from my Father I have made known to you" (John 15:15).

In His words, Jesus pointed out that those who began as His followers had matured into individuals capable of stepping up into the leadership roles to which they were called. Jesus prepared His followers for their seasons of leadership.

- A few minutes of brutal honesty regarding your motives as a leader are worth years of self-deception. How are you preparing those you lead to become peak performers?

_____

_____

Key Concepts
- How you respond to feedback on the results of your leadership is a powerful indicator of your leadership motives. It will be a key factor in what others tell you and how they perceive your true values.
- Preparing the next generation of leaders is a far more long-lasting element of your leadership legacy than the performance results you accomplished during your own season of leadership.

A Point to Ponder
If your first reaction to negative feedback regarding your leadership style is denial or hurt feelings, you may need to ask yourself, "What is it about the negative feedback that hurts so much?" On the other hand, if you are fixated on receiving positive feedback and hunger for more and more of it, you should probably ask yourself what is feeding that need for praise. In both cases, the answer will most likely involve your pride.

Next Steps
Today as you go about your business, review the first two tests of a servant leader:

1. Welcoming and wanting _____.
   How can you make this test a reality in your leadership roles?

2. _____ when your season of leadership is past. What are you doing to prepare for this transition?

week two

day two | **2** • •

How Do We Edge God Out?

Quote for Today

When a man is wrapped up in himself, he makes a pretty small package.[2]

John Ruskin

What God's Word Says

Then Jesus came from Galilee to the Jordan to be baptized by John. But John tried to deter him, saying, "I need to be baptized by you, and do you come to me?" Jesus replied, "Let it be so now; it is proper for us to do this to fulfill all righteousness." Then John consented. As soon as Jesus was baptized, he went up out of the water. At that moment heaven was opened, and he saw the Spirit of God descending like a dove and lighting on him. And a voice from heaven said, "This is my Son, whom I love; with him I am well pleased." (Matt. 3:13–17)

Pause and Reflect

• What does the passage above reveal about the heart of a servant leader?

_____

_____

• How can you become more like Jesus in your approach to leadership?

_____

_____

A Prayer for Today

Perfect Example, Selfless One, You showed me how to live and lead as a servant and yet it seems so difficult, so hard to do. Patiently walk with me as I demonstrate for others the qualities of servant leadership, so that they, too, might learn to walk in them. In Jesus's Name, Amen!

Today's Topic
How Do We Edge God Out?

How do you define "ego?" We toss around the word referring to how important a person believes he or she is. Let's be really honest—some people apparently overestimate how much the rest of us need them on the planet.

Think about it for a moment. What do the following actions say about a person's attitude toward himself or herself?

- Using the emergency lane to bypass traffic congestion.
- Taking a week's grocery shopping through the *6 Items or Less* express check-out.
- Parking on top of the *Fire Lane – No Parking* markings for a quick trip to the ATM.
- Using one's position and influence for personal gain.

You get the picture.

There never has been anyone who deserved to think more highly of Himself than Jesus. Yet Scripture shows a humility and servant attitude that was uncommon in His day and remains uncommon today. Jesus could have demanded respect, honor, and social accolades, but He refused to lead by fear and intimidation.

Look Inside

Today we want to help you check yourself on the third test of servant leadership:

Test 3: *Control*

Do you let God be the Leader and you the servant? The term *leader* (or *leaders*) is mentioned only six times in the King James Version of the Bible, while *servant* (or *servants*) is mentioned more than nine hundred times. That very fact underlines the truth that forms our third test: *God is not looking for leaders but for servants who will let Him be their Leader.*

When God approached Abraham, He had the plan and Abraham was to carry it out according to God's promise. When God approached Moses, He provided leadership for the shy, withdrawn man. When God approached David, it was not to ask him to lead but to ask him to serve using his harp, slingshot, and sword.

When God was the Leader, things worked out well for the men above. Well, of course, that means things worked according to God's plan. However, replacing God's leadership with self-directed leadership led to chaos. **E**dging **G**od **O**ut, or EGO, always has disastrous consequences. If we want life to work out, we must recognize that it is all about God, not us.

What Is Your Leadership EGO?

In this study, we're not talking about a psychological term; we're talking about an issue of the heart. Here are two ways to define the EGO difference of self-serving and servant leaders.

For Self-Serving Leaders: or   For Servant Leaders:

EGO: Edging God Out   EGO: Exalting God Only

It doesn't get much simpler than that.

Let's take another look at the Scripture passage with which we began today's reading.

> Then Jesus came from Galilee to the Jordan to be baptized by John. But John tried to deter him, saying, "I need to be baptized by you, and do you come to me?" Jesus replied, "Let it be so now; it is proper for us to do this to fulfill all righteousness." Then John consented. As soon as Jesus was baptized, he went up out of the water. At that moment heaven was opened, and he saw the Spirit of God descending like a dove and lighting on him. And a voice from heaven said, "This is my Son, whom I love; with him I am well pleased." (Matt. 3:13–17)

Jesus demonstrated two very significant attributes of servant leadership in His interaction with His cousin, John the Baptist. (1) He validated and affirmed John in his ministry, and (2) He didn't ask His followers to do anything He wasn't willing to do. Servant leaders never ask anyone to do something they aren't willing to do themselves!

Look Inside

Look at the EGO diagram below. At the top are three ways we edge God out. Today we will take a closer look at each of these three attitudes.

Edging God Out as

• Whom I worship
• My source of security and self-worth
• My audience, my ultimate authority and my judge

Pride

An overly high opinion of yourself, exaggerated esteem of self, haughtiness, arrogance

"Thinking more of and about yourself than you should."
Romans 12:3

Fear

An insecure view of the future producing self-protection.

"The Fear of man is a trap ...."
Proverbs 29:25

Promoting Self
• Boasting
• Taking all of the credit
• Showing off
• Doing all the talking
• Demanding all the attention

Protecting Self
• Hiding behind position
• Withholding information
• Intimidating others
• Hoarding control and revenues
• Discouraging honest feedback

Always separates
man from God, other people, and himself or herself
Always compares
with others and is never happy
Always distorts
the truth into a false sense of security or fear

1. You Edge God Out When You Put Something Else in God's Place as the Object of Your Worship.

Your priority is your god; it's that simple. Whenever anything becomes more important to you than God, you are in effect bowing to it, adoring it, or giving yourself to it. In short, you worship it. This can take many forms. It might be an object such as money, a house, a car, or a business. It might be a desire for power, recognition, or appreciation. It might be a habit that edges God out—running, watching television or movies, eating, or sleeping. Here's the tough part. From the list below, circle any attitude, action, or possession that could potentially become a life-focus for you. Be honest!

Money	Cars	Clothes
Desire for power	Appreciation	Popularity
Running	Reading	Eating or Cooking
Working on your house	Work	Boating
Public recognition	Fame	Success
Gardening	Watching television/movies	Sleeping

• What do you need to do to keep your attitude toward these things in check?

_____

_____

_____

• Consider for a moment how you make leadership decisions. From the list below, circle anything that might become more important to you than God:

Your boss's opinion	Influence of fellow workers
Your money involved	Fear of failure
Potential promotion	Showing up coworkers

Power, recognition, appreciation, money—whatever it is, it's not worth it if it takes the place of your worship of God. Paul had the following words for the Philippians: "For we who worship God in the Spirit ... put no confidence in human effort. Instead, we boast about what Christ Jesus has done for us" (Phil. 3:3 NLT).

2. You Edge God Out When You Rely on Other Sources for Your Security and Sufficiency.

One of the greatest temptations is to rely on yourself instead of on God until you are at your wit's end. When you trust in something other than the unconditional love of God, other than in His care for you, you edge God out. When you put your security in other things—your intellect, your position, your business contacts, your talent, anything—you are counting on the temporal instead of the eternal.

"Trust in the Lord with all your heart and lean not on your own understanding; in all your ways acknowledge him, and he will make your paths straight" (Prov 3:5–6).

- Sometimes you rely on other things or other people to get you out of trouble. Check any of the items below that you have ever relied on as your security:

_____ Money	_____ Business contacts	_____ Experience
_____ Intellect	_____ Education	_____ Position

- Circle any of the above items on which you are now relying.

Anything you count on instead of God is temporal rather than eternal. Your security should be in the unconditional love of God and in His care for you.

"Cast all your anxiety on him because he cares for you" (1 Pet. 5:7).

3. You Edge God Out When You Put Others in His Place as Your Primary Audience.

If your self-worth or security is based on what others think, then you don't have much security. In Robert S. McGee's *The Search for Significance,* we learn that if the devil could get you to buy into a formula for self-worth, it would be: Your self-worth = your performance + the opinions of others.

If you constantly base your self-worth on your performance or the opinions of others, you're always going to be chasing an elusive, frustrating fantasy. All the world is a stage and God is the audience of One.

"Whatever you do, work at it with all your heart, as working for the Lord, not for men" (Col. 3:23). Not only is God the Audience you are to please, He is the Judge of all the earth. He determines your destiny. How many businessmen or even church leaders thought they were getting away with devious deals only to discover that God makes known from the housetops the secrets that were whispered in the closet! Your character is revealed when no one is watching. But there is a catch—God is *always* watching! He is your perpetual audience of one . . . the One you honor above all.

- Read Matthew 4:1-11 and list the ways Jesus resisted the temptation to Edge God Out.

_____

_____

_____

_____

_____

_____

_____

_____

_____

_____

It is easy to concentrate too much on the physical hardships of Jesus's fasting experience in the wilderness and miss the profound spiritual conditioning for servant leadership that took place. Jesus faced three of the most universal and powerful temptations a leader can face:

1. Instant gratification

2. Recognition and applause

3. Improper use of and lust for power

Because Jesus faced these temptations from the spiritual perspective, He was able to overcome them. Too many leaders negate the power of God when they face worldly temptations. In every season of leadership you enter, you will be faced with temptations. The quality of your service will be a direct result of your spiritual preparation.

 ## Look Inside

List a few examples of how you have faced the following temptations:

• Instant self-gratification:

_____

_____

• Recognition and applause of others:

_____

_____

• Improper use of your power and influence

_____

_____

Notice that Jesus used His knowledge of God's Word to confront and defeat Satan's temptations. This is one example of the importance of memorizing Scripture.

 ## Key Concepts

• The hearts of self-serving leaders Edge God Out by putting something in God's place as the object of their worship, trusting in something else for their security and self-worth and valuing someone else's opinion more than God's.

• When you Edge God Out you end up putting your faith and trust in people and things that are always at risk and are never a hundred percent reliable.

• Satan's formula for self-worth is that self-worth is the product of what you have, what you do, and what other people think of you. If you adopt this formula, you will live an always-anxious, always-unfulfilled life and lead others to do the same.

A Point to Ponder

Edging God Out is usually not a violent act of the will. It is the subtle movement over time of self onto the throne of your life, through little acts of pride and fear. What choices will you make today that may give you a sense who is on the throne of your life?

_____

_____

_____

_____

_____

_____

_____

_____

Next Steps

• Today, what do you think will be your greatest temptation to Edge God Out and act like a self-serving leader?

_____

_____

• How will you deal with the temptation?

_____

_____

• What are the dangers of giving in?

_____

_____

• What are the benefits of resisting the temptation through God's power?

_____

_____

Tomorrow we will ask you to describe any situation in which you were tempted to be a self-serving leader and how you handled the temptation.

week two

day three | 3 • • •

PRIDE EDGES GOD OUT

66 Quote for Today

When false pride and toxic fear enter into a relationship, they poison it. When they become the driving force in our leadership decisions, they render them ineffective.[3]

Ken Blanchard and Phil Hodges

What God's Word Says

". . . Let not the wise man boast of his wisdom or the strong man boast of his strength or the rich man boast of his riches, but let him who boasts boast about this: that he understands and knows me, that I am the Lord, who exercises kindness, justice and righteousness on earth, for in these I delight," declares the Lord. (Jer. 9:23–24)

⏸ Pause and Reflect

Describe a time when you have been tempted to boast about yourself or your accomplishments. What should be the object of your boasting?

_____

_____

_____

_____

_____

_____

_____

A Prayer for Today

Lord, help me see the destructive impact of my pride on the quality of my leadership and my relationships with the people I care about and with you. In Jesus's Name, Amen!

Today's Topic
PRIDE EDGES GOD OUT

In the first two days of this week, you were been given three tests to determine the level of your servant leadership. Review Week 2, Day 1 and Week 2, Day 2 and complete the following descriptions of the first three tests.

- **Test 1:** Do you _____ and want _____?
- **Test 2**: Are you preparing a _____ for when your season of _____ _____ is complete?
- **Test 3:** Do you let God be the _____ and you the_____?

Look Inside

Today we want to help you check yourself on the fourth test of servant leadership.

Test 4: *React or Respond*

When you are treated like a servant, do you respond like a servant? Self-serving leaders *react* to things that happen to them. They are almost a stimulus-response machine. If you say or do something that hooks their pride or fear, they react. Servant leaders, on the other hand, *respond* to things that happen to them. Their responses are led by their interactions and motivations to serve.

- What is your reaction when you are asked to do something that is "below" you?

    _____ Why did you ask me to do that?

    _____ Why don't you do it yourself?

    _____ I have more important things to do.

    _____ Anybody could do that!

    _____ I don't have time to do things like that.

    _____ Other: _____

Self-serving leaders don't like being bossed around, taken for granted, or treated as inferior. However, if you are a servant you aren't offended when someone treats you like one. A servant leader always is ready to respond as a servant would.

The Dynamics of Pride

Pride centers on the promotion of self. It is, as we read in Romans 12:3, thinking of yourself *more highly than you ought*. Here are some of the ways you can tell that pride is at its destructive work.

Put a check mark next to any of the following demonstrations of pride them seem familiar:

_____ When you are engaged in a discussion, you resist admitting that the other person's idea is actually better than your own. In other words, "The righter they sound, the madder you get."

_____ You start to do all the talking, taking too much credit, demanding all the attention, boasting, showing off, or demanding service on the basis of your position.

_____ You judge the value of an idea by who said it rather than by the quality of the thought.

_____ You treat people as too far below you in position or credentials to seek out their input on issues that affect them.

_____ Your image becomes more important than substance and truth.

_____ You act as if the rules, judgments, and standards you impose on others should not apply to you because of who you are or the position you hold.

_____ Your compensation becomes more important as a mark of success than the ethical and relational price you paid to attain it.

_____ Winning and losing become the only criteria you value and character becomes an option.

_____ You look in the mirror to find the source of all success and out the window for the cause of failure.

Key Concepts

- Pride blinds and cripples leadership at all levels of human relationship. It sets self-interest and self-promotion above service and community. In doing its ugly work, it denies the truth, and opens both leaders and followers to manipulation and exploitation.

- When you are tempted to make decisions out of pride, you need to ask, _Do I really want to make a decision based on my over-inflated perception of myself?_ You can be sure that pride-based decisions won't give you the best long-term results. You might get a mile or so down the road, but such decisions won't see you through the entire trip.

A Point to Ponder

Acting out of pride is like trying to blow up a balloon with a hole in it. It is a lonely business, requiring consistent effort with only temporary results that never satisfy or please anyone.

Next Steps

Look for hints that pride is working its way into the decisions you make. Reread the Scripture from today's study and let the truth of God's Word guide your thoughts and actions.

As you go through your day, review the four tests for a servant leader. Recognize how your awareness of the characteristics of a servant leader affects your thinking and behavior during the day.

week two

day four | 4 • • • •

FEAR – A GOOD THING TURNED BAD

Quote for Today

No passion so effectually robs the mind of all its powers of acting and reasoning as fear.[4]

Edmund Burke

What God's Word Says

"The fear of the Lord is the beginning of wisdom . . ." (Ps. 111:10).

"Do not be anxious about anything, but in everything, by prayer and petition, with thanksgiving present your request to God. And the peace of God, which transcends all understanding, will guard your hearts and your minds in Christ Jesus" (Phil. 4:6–7).

Pause and Reflect

Whom do you really fear most—God or man? Why?

_____

_____

_____

_____

_____

_____

_____

A Prayer for Today

Father God, fearing You seems scary to me. I want to be in reverential awe of You, knowing that You hold life in the balance. I desire to choose rightly today so that I, too, might be capable of acts of courage for those I influence. In Jesus's Name, Amen!

Today's Topic
FEAR — A GOOD THING TURNED BAD

Review the four tests of a servant leader by completing the statements below:

- **Test 1:** Do you _____ and want _____ ?

- **Test 2:** Are you preparing a _____ for when your season of _____ _____ is complete?

- **Test 3:** Do you let God be the _____ and you be the _____?

- **Test 4:** When you are treated like a _____ , do you _____ like a _____?

Jesus said: "But I will show you whom you should fear: Fear him who, after the killing of the body, has power to throw you into hell. Yes, I tell you, fear him" (Luke 12:5).

Sometimes our fear is misplaced—we fear the wrong thing. That's what Jesus was talking about in the passage above. His audience apparently redirected its fear from God, who is worthy of fear, to man.

Sometimes our sense of self-worth is based on how much fear we can create in the lives of those we lead. Today, we will help you evaluate yourself on the fifth test of servant leadership.

Test 5: *Fear*

Do you lead out of your own fear or create fear for those you lead? The spiritual contest between fearing God and fearing man is nothing new or any less intense today than when it was played out in the lives of the heroes of the Bible. Heroes who performed monumental acts of courage also fell victim to the temptations of fear.

- Read the following Scripture passages and identify the biblical heroes who succumbed to their fear:

- Genesis 12:10-20: _____ lied about his relationship with his wife to save his own life.

- Exodus 4:10-17: _____ pleaded with God to send someone else to talk to Pharaoh about releasing the Jews, because he felt inadequate as a public speaker.

- 2 Samuel 11:1-18: _____ tried to cover up his infidelity by having Bathsheba's husband killed.

- Matthew 26:69-75: _____ denied knowing Jesus at the time of His arrest.

Like the biblical heroes above, we often fail to trust God as a secure and sufficient supply of unconditional love and safety. Fear makes it easy for us to edge God out as the focus of our worship, as our source of security and self-worth, and as our only audience and judge. When we start to edge God out in our daily decision-making, things start to happen that are not consistent with being a servant leader.

We are most likely to be fearful when we are heavily dependent on sources of security and measurements of self-worth that are temporary and always at risk. In the previous session we agreed that we have an ego problem—addicted to self, fear, and pride. An addiction is an ever-increasing desire for something that has an ever-decreasing ability to satisfy. The total focus of addictive behavior is to maintain a secure source of supply.

So what makes us addicted to self? The answer lies in our addictive dependence on unreliable, always-at-risk sources of security and self-worth. Poorly grounded foundations of self-esteem and security inject lethal levels of toxic fear and self-protection into our relationships. When we are addicted to self, our fear can become toxic and poison our lives and the lives of people around us. This is especially true when we fear that the source fueling our addictions is at risk.

 ## Look Inside

Evaluate your levels of fear and your reliance on inadequate sources of security and self-worth. In answering each question, be completely honest with yourself. This questionnaire is for your awareness; not for sharing with other people.

Questionnaire

1. To what degree do you gain security from the following? (One is the lowest; five is the highest.)

Applause	1 | 2 | 3 | 4 | 5	Relationships	1 | 2 | 3 | 4 | 5
Money	1 | 2 | 3 | 4 | 5	Knowledge & Intellect	1 | 2 | 3 | 4 | 5
Busyness	1 | 2 | 3 | 4 | 5	Health & Fitness	1 | 2 | 3 | 4 | 5
Performance	1 | 2 | 3 | 4 | 5	Physical appearance	1 | 2 | 3 | 4 | 5
Sex	1 | 2 | 3 | 4 | 5	Style & Fashion	1 | 2 | 3 | 4 | 5
Mystery	1 | 2 | 3 | 4 | 5	Position & Power	1 | 2 | 3 | 4 | 5
Credentials	1 | 2 | 3 | 4 | 5	Heritage & History	1 | 2 | 3 | 4 | 5

2. Which of the following fears tend to negatively affect your relationships? Check all that apply:

Fear of . . .

___ rejection	___ job loss	___ loss of control
___ inadequacy	___ competition	___ the future
___ failure	___ success	___ disclosure
___ change	___ exclusion	___ obsolescence
___ loneliness	___ criticism	___ intimacy
___ retaliation		

3. How do you deal with the following situations? Check to indicate your response.

	out of confidence	out of fear
Imperfect people and relationships	____	____
Fallible organizations & institutions	____	____
Material assets	____	____
Obsolescent skills, information, & knowledge	____	____
Luck and good intentions	____	____
Past successes and future actions	____	____

Key Concepts

- The capacity to fear is a gift from God. The Bible tells us that "fear of the Lord is the beginning of wisdom" (Ps. 111:10). When applied as God intended, fear can keep us focused on doing the right thing for the right reasons. Yet when we turn it into the fear of one another, we forfeit its benefits and make it into a joy-stealing source of pain and loneliness.

- Instead of enhancing life as a dimension of keeping our focus on God, fear has poisoned human relationships ever since man first stepped out of God's will. The first thing Adam and Eve did after they ate the forbidden fruit was become self-conscious, cover up, and hide in fear. In a way we have been hiding ever since, in fear that our weaknesses and bad behavior will be found out. The irony is that God—the only one who matters on an eternal scale—already sees and knows it all.

A Point to Ponder

Think of a time when fear of rejection or failure prevented you from doing or saying something that might have helped a friend avoid an impending mistake. What excuse did you give yourself to justify letting your fears control your inaction? Was it worth it?

_____

_____

Next Steps

Now that you understand more about how fear affects you and those you lead, what will you do differently today?

_____

_____

_____

ALTARING YOUR EGO TO EXALT GOD ONLY

Quote for Today

God expects of us the one thing that glorifies Him—and that is to remain absolutely confident in Him, remembering what He has said beforehand, and sure that His purposes will be fulfilled.[5]

Oswald Chambers

What God's Word Says

"Peace I leave with you. My peace I give to you. I do not give to you as the world gives. Your heart must not be troubled or fearful. You have heard Me tell you, "I am going away and I am coming to you." If you loved me, you would have rejoiced that I am going to My Father, because the Father is greater than I. (John 14:27–28 NKJV)

Pause and Reflect

Being troubled and fearful cancels out peace. Jesus took refuge in His knowledge of God's love. When you are troubled and fearful, in what do you take refuge? Explain your response.

_____

_____

_____

_____

A Prayer for Today

Jesus loves me this I know for the Bible tells me so! Thanks for the reminder of this simple song to teach me a truth that Jesus knew from before the beginning of time. May I apply these same thoughts to my every day decisions and thereby demonstrate confidence in the One who loves me. In Jesus's Loving Name, Amen!

Today's Topic
ALTARING YOUR EGO TO EXALT GOD ONLY

- Describe a time when you have experienced unexplainable peace in the midst of a tumultuous situation.

  _____

  _____

- What promises did you see God fulfill during your time of trouble?

  _____

  _____

Jesus was comforting His followers because human nature cannot grasp the concept of powerful humility. Yet, another attribute of a heart that Exalts God Only is steady God-grounded confidence. Jesus's confidence in God empowered Him to stick to the task—to the point that He was crucified. Even then, He had confidence in God's plan!

Look Inside

Reflect on your spiritual ups and downs over the past week or so. Plot your spiritual confidence as evidenced by your thoughts and actions.

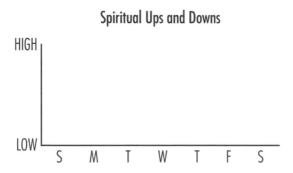

If you are like most people, your spiritual confidence isn't represented by a relatively straight line in the high range. Instead, you probably are more like me—a series of ups and downs that are grounded in my circumstances more than in my spiritual confidence.

What are your options when you encounter troubling situations? Well, you can deny them and pretend they don't exist or you can deal with them by reminding yourself that God is in control. People will disappoint you; God never will. So, when you encounter troubling situations you must intentionally remember God's promises.

God's promises provide peace in the midst of life's chaos. God never promised we would be immune from problems; He simply promised to sustain us through them. How can you be sustained through life's troubles?

_____

_____

Change Your Perspective

Think about your spiritual perspective. By nature, you see things from a human perspective. You try to develop self-confidence that will empower you through the ups and downs of life. Sometimes you amaze yourself with your inner strength; other times you disappoint yourself with your actions. So goes life based on self-confidence.

Later, however, you begin a faith relationship with God through Jesus Christ. Your perspective on life changes and you begin to see parts of life from God's point of view. But when life gets tough you have a relapse and begin to trust yourself to deal with the situation. You have faith in God, but you respond from a perspective that is inconsistent with your faith. The casual observer sees you as hypocritical.

So, how do you change your perspective? When humility and God-grounded confidence guide your life, your perspective changes. The problem is that many times our confidence is grounded in everything except God.

• From the list below, check the things in which you might place confidence.

_____ education	_____ position	_____ intelligence
_____ money	_____ personality	_____ relationships
_____ possessions	_____ appearance	_____ other: _____

• What can you do to keep from placing your confidence in the items you checked?

_____

_____

_____

God-grounded confidence doesn't come easy; it must be an intentional choice of your daily life. Every day you must recommit yourself to God-grounded confidence. This means refusing to edge God out by choosing to exalt God only. It's a battle . . . a daily battle!

Humility isn't easily developed. Consider the following definitions of humility:

> *People of humility don't think less of themselves, they just think about themselves less.*[6]
>
> Ken Blanchard and Norman Vincent Peale

> *People with humility don't deny their power; they just recognize that it passes through them and from them.*[7]
>
> Fred Smith

As a leadership trait, humility is a heart attitude that reflects a keen understanding of your limitations as a leader to accomplish something on your own. It gives credit to forces other than your own brilliance or effort when a victory is won or an obstacle overcome. According to Jim Collins in his book *Good to Great,* a leader with a humble heart looks out the window to find and applaud the true causes for success and in the mirror to find and accept responsibility for failure.

Leading like Jesus requires humbly receiving and honoring the nonnegotiable boundaries He has set for accomplishing true and lasting results. Jesus said, "I am the vine; you are the branches. If a man remains in me and I in him, he will bear much fruit; apart from me you can do nothing" (John 15:5).

There is a difference between putting on the appearance of humility and being truly humbled in the presence of God. True humility is being brutally honest about yourself. It is seeing yourself as God sees you. You are not to be piously humble about what He has given you or arrogantly proud of what you have or have done.

The humility Jesus demonstrated did not arise from the lack of self-esteem, love, power, or ability. His humility came from the fact that He knew who He was, where He came from, where He was going, and who was backing Him. In fact, that is the point—knowing all this He humbled Himself and became a servant. For more than three years He had taught servant leadership to His disciples, but they never could quite grasp it. Then at the end of His earthly ministry He demonstrated humility in a way that would touch their hearts and burn a picture of true humility into their minds.

> It was just before the Passover Feast. Jesus knew that the time had come for him to leave this world and go to the Father. Having loved his own who were in the world, he now showed them the full extent of his love. The evening meal was being served, and the devil had already prompted Judas Iscariot, son of Simon, to betray Jesus. Jesus knew that the Father had put all things under his power, and that He had come for God and was returning to God (John 13:1–3).

In contrast to what Jesus knew, Peter didn't get it! Take a look at John 13:4-11:

> So he got up from the meal, took off his outer clothing, and wrapped a towel around his waist. After that, he poured water into a basin and began to wash his disciples' feet, drying them with the towel that was wrapped around him. He came to Simon Peter, who said to him, "Lord, are You going to wash my feet?" Jesus replied, "You do not realize now what I am doing, but later you will understand." "No," said Peter, "You shall never wash my feet." Jesus answered, "Unless I wash you, you have no part with me."
>
> "Then, Lord," Simon Peter replied, "not just my feet but my hands and my head as well!" Jesus answered, "A person who has had a bath needs only to wash his feet; his whole body is clean. And you are clean, though not every one of you." For he knew who was going to betray him, and that was why he said not every one was clean.

- What did Peter *not* understand (check all that apply)?

_____ where Jesus came from

_____ Jesus's relationship with the Father

_____ who Jesus was

_____ what Jesus was doing

_____ why Jesus was washing his feet

We can see that Peter did not understand what Jesus was doing or why Jesus was washing his feet.

Take a look at the passage below and determine what Jesus was teaching His disciples.

> When he had finished washing their feet, he put on his clothes and returned to his place. "Do you understand what I have done for you?" he asked them. "You call me 'Teacher' and 'Lord,' and rightly so, for that is what I am Now that I, your Lord and Teacher, have washed your feet, you also should wash one another's feet. I have set you an example that you should do as I have done for you. I tell you the truth, no servant is greater than his master, nor is a messenger greater than the one who sent him. Now that you know these things, you will be blessed if you do them. (John 13:12–17)

How can you serve someone today as a demonstration of your servant heart and humility?

_____

_____

_____

_____

_____

Key Concepts

- Embrace a perspective of the here and now in light of eternity.
- Seek to lead for a higher purpose—beyond success, beyond significance—to obedience and surrendered sacrifice.
- Scrupulously assess my level of trust and surrender to what I believe about God, His kingdom, and His claim on my life and leadership.

A Point to Ponder

To successfully combat the temptation to be self-serving in your leadership, every day you must put your EGO on the altar and Exalt God Only.

Next Steps

Think about some ways you can serve others today from a genuinely humble heart. In the space provided below, list the first name of the person you plan to serve and how you plan to serve him or her.

Name	Action	Response

Tomorrow, revisit the list above and record how the individuals responded.

_____

_____

_____

_____

_____

week three

THE *HEAD* OF A SERVANT LEADER

3

Memory Verse for the Week

*"Do not conform any longer
to the pattern of this world,
but be transformed by the
renewing of your mind.
Then you will be able to test
and approve what God's will is—
his good, pleasing and perfect will"
(Rom. 12:2).*

As followers of Jesus, we must seek to lead like Jesus in this world. As a philosophy of leadership, servant leadership may be considered one option among many others; but as a theology of leadership, it is a mandate for all who call Jesus Lord. Foundational to tapping into the essence of leading like Jesus is embracing a life purpose of loving and serving God and people.

People and organizations work more effectively if clear vision and values are established up front. Unethical leadership is often the result of the moral confusion created by an organization's lack of clearly established guidelines, which a compelling vision provides. That's exactly where servant leadership begins.

Is the problem confined to business? No! Being more ethical and values-driven benefits families, churches, community organizations and any relationship in which we influence others. Leading like Jesus is for everyone, everywhere.

Maybe you've heard someone say, "It's all in your head" in response to a fear or perceived situation. Leadership is also in your head. Paul told the Romans that transformation begins in the mind. This week we will take a closer look at the mental aspects of leadership.

3 week three
day one | 1 •

WHOM ARE YOU FOLLOWING?

" Quote for Today
Leadership is about going somewhere. Effective leadership begins with a clear vision, whether for your personal life, your family, or an organization. If your followers don't know where you are going and where you are trying to take them, they will have a hard time getting excited about the journey.[1]

Ken Blanchard and Phil Hodges

What God's Word Says
"Where there is no vision, the people are unrestrained" (Prov. 29:18 NASB).

Pause and Reflect
What is the source of your vision?

_____ my imagination

_____ other people's thoughts

_____ my relationship with God

_____ I don't have a vision

_____ other: _____

A Prayer for Today
Lord, let me remember that Your vision is the only one that succeeds. Give me a vision for my personal and professional life that is so strong that it will overwhelm me and excite those I love and lead. In Jesus's Name, Amen!

Today's Topic
WHOM ARE YOU FOLLOWING?
Surrendering your heart to Jesus is the first step toward servant leadership. The heart repre-

sents your motivations. But simply being motivated isn't enough. At some point, your motivation must travel to your head where it affects your beliefs and perspectives.

Too many people try to change their opinions without ever addressing their points of view. That is the equivalent of painting over rust—a temporary surface solution to a deeper issue. There are people who have favorable opinions of God, but they have not let His truth penetrate their points of view. Likewise, there are plenty of resources that will challenge your opinion of leadership issues, but the real issue isn't your opinion; it's your point of view.

• If someone developed his or her attitude about leadership from watching you lead, what would he or she conclude it means to be a leader?

_____

_____

Every great leader has a specific concept of leadership that sets the boundaries for influential relationships. Jesus modeled leadership activities that were representative of His leadership point of view, which was a byproduct of His habits. Jesus fully aligned Himself with God's instructions. Therefore, Jesus had God's point of view. As a result, the public Jesus was just an authentic reflection of His relationship with God.

That's where too many of today's leaders miss the mark. They lack God's point of view because they don't take advantage of their opportunities to develop godly habits of mind. Servant leadership isn't leadership without control; it is Jesus's way of doing things.

• Respond to these questions:

1. Did Jesus try to please everyone?

2. Did Jesus ever compromise His values or morals?

3. Did Jesus ever value popularity?

The answers to these questions paint a succinct picture of Jesus's leadership point of view. Of course, His leadership point of view stands in direct contrast to many of today's leadership points of view. Yet, in many situations, today's leadership model has caused more harm than good!

Jesus focused only on pleasing God, His audience of One. That meant preaching the gospel of salvation in places where He wasn't welcomed. He showed His disciples what it meant to lead, and then sent them out to share the Good News with people everywhere.

Jesus asked His followers to do things that were not socially acceptable. He asked them to live by values that put them at odds with society's trends—and He expects the same today. He told His followers that they would be persecuted for telling people what they did not want to hear. If His disciples would have adopted the world's point of view, Jesus's expectations would have gone unmet. Even those who knew Him personally struggled to live up to His model of leadership.

Two Parts of Leadership

Jesus clearly demonstrated two parts of leadership:

1. A visionary role—doing the right thing with a focus on results.

2. An implementation role—doing things right with a focus on people.

Some people think leadership is all about the visionary role while management is about implementation. When such a distinction is made, management always seems to get a second-class status compared to visionary leadership. We prefer not to distinguish between the two, and as a result, the visionary and implementation roles will both be thought of as leadership roles during this study. These two roles of leadership are directly related to how you view results and people.

Look Inside

- Describe a situation in which you have been trying to accomplish a specific goal by working with other people.

  _____

  _____

- Evaluate your personal emphasis on results and people in this leadership effort. Make an X on the line below to indicate to what degree results or people are getting the greater emphasis.

  Results _____People

Your Leadership Point of View

- Have you ever thought about your leadership point of view? How do you view the role of a leader, and what do you think are a leader's responsibilities? How should a leader act? How should a leader relate to people with whom he or she works?

  _____

  _____

- If your leadership point of view involves your responses to the questions above, what is your leadership point of view?

  _____

  _____

- Take a few minutes and write your philosophy for leading in an organization

  _____

  _____

  _____

- Now write your leadership point of view for leading in a family.

  _____

  _____

  _____

- How do these to statements differ (if they do) and why?

  _____

  _____

Jesus's Leadership Point of View

Let's see how Jesus handled the two leadership roles—vision and implementation.

Below are descriptions of the vision and implementation roles of leadership. Underline the word or phrase in each list that best describes the essence of the concept.

Visionary

- Seeing the vision with an eternal purpose
- Painting a compelling picture of the future
- Defining and modeling the operating values, structure, and behavior norms of your organization

Implementation

- Serving the ongoing needs of those involved in doing the work
- Creating the follower environment that inspires commitment to the vision
- Elevating the growth and development of people from a means to an end goal
- Developing a level of intimacy with the needs and aspirations of the people with whom you work or live

The remainder of this week's study will focus on some specific aspects of the leadership role. In the end, you will develop a clear understanding of the difference between leadership success and effectiveness. *Success* can involve accomplishing short-term goals that are detrimental to the people responsible for meeting the long-term goals. *Effectiveness* seeks to meet the long-term objectives while creating an atmosphere that contributes to the personal growth of the individuals.

- In terms of your drive for success or effectiveness, how would you characterize your leadership skills?

_____

_____

Key Concepts

Three truths about high-level leadership:

1. Effective leadership depends on whom you follow.

2. Sustainable servant leadership behaviors only emerge as an expression of a committed and convicted heart.

3. As with all comprehensive theories of leadership, in leading like Jesus the doing is the hard part.

A Point to Ponder

The message before us of Jesus, seeking to serve as He gave that principle of taking a towel and water and washing his disciples' feet, was not to put our interest ahead of others. In so doing, that message was very simple. His deeds and His words matched. It was a message of love and forgiveness for those who would believe and follow Him—a message of transformation, a message of hope, of eternal hope.

- Bill Pollard, Chairman Emeritus, ServiceMaster Company

Next Steps

Think about your leadership point of view today and commit to follow Jesus as your leadership role model and practice servant leadership.

DEVELOPING YOUR VISION AS A SERVANT LEADER

Quote for Today

Vision is the world's most desperate need. There are no hopeless situations, only people who think hopelessly.[2]

Winifred Newman

What God's Word Says

So then, men ought to regard us as servants of Christ and as those entrusted with the secret things of God. Now it is required that those who have been given a trust must prove faithful. (1 Cor. 4:1–2)

Pause and Reflect

How does the passage above compare to the world's concept of success?

_____

_____

A Prayer for Today

Father God, clarify my vision of the future. Help me know and respond to what you hold most important in the lives of those I lead and where you would have us go together. In Jesus's Name, Amen!

Today's Topic
DEVELOPING YOUR VISION AS A SERVANT LEADER

You've heard it said—*No organization will rise above the passion of its leader.* Servant leadership begins with a clear and compelling vision of the future that excites passion in the leader and commitment in those who follow. That's the kind of leader Jesus was. Jesus didn't expect His followers to get excited about something He was lethargic about. Instead, He lived His passion and His followers, therefore, were equipped for their future roles of leadership.

The Leadership Vision

Effective leadership begins with a clear vision, whether you are talking about your personal life or the life of an organization. In practical terms, a compelling vision has three parts, which an effective leader must be able to communicate.[3]

1. Your purpose: Where are you headed and why?

2. Your picture of the future: What will your future look like if you are accomplishing your purpose? What will be accomplished if you succeed?

3. Your values: What do you stand for? On what principles will you make your ongoing decisions?

A compelling vision tells who you are, where you are going, and what will guide your journey. Let's begin by looking at how our vision relates to our personal lives as leaders.

Clarifying Your Personal Vision

Before seeking to influence the thinking and behavior of others, it is important to have a sense of your own personal vision. Who are you? What is your purpose? Where are you going? How do you picture the future for yourself? What will guide your journey? What are your personal values? In helping you develop a clear statement of your own personal vision, we will use the personal vision that Ken Blanchard developed for himself.

Writing Your Own Purpose/Mission Statement

A purpose/mission statement tells you who you are and identifies your purpose on earth. Richard Bolles, in his best-selling book *What Color Is Your Parachute?*, suggests that there are three parts to writing a personal mission statement.[4] The first two are goals that every person should pursue, while the third is individually unique.

The first part of any mission statement is becoming more aware of what God is doing and wants to do in your life. Bolles says you cannot talk about your *calling* unless you talk about the *Caller*.

The second part of a personal mission statement is to identify the impact your life will have on the world. If you ask people whether they want to make the world a better place, they all say yes. But when you ask them how they plan to make the world a better place, they stare blankly as if you're speaking a foreign language. The way to make the world a better place is through your moment-to-moment activities. Every day is full of opportunities to make the world a better place as you interact with people.

The third and final aspect of a mission statement is unique to you. What is it you do that, when you do it, you lose track of time? That probably is why you are here on earth. The Lord did not put you here to fight against yourself; He put you together with a unique set of gifts and abilities so that people can see Him through the things you do.

Look Inside

- From the personal characteristics listed below, circle the ones that you believe are strong points for you:

energy	enthusiasm	creativity
sense of humor	patience	people skills
good looks	servant attitude	listening
charm/wit	artistic ability	communicating
physical strength	happiness	other: _____

- Use some of the verbs in the list below to write a statement describing how you interact with people:

teach	love	sell
study	plan	speak
manage	encourage	care
produce	help	build
lead	act	convince
motivate	stimulate	write
educate	inspire	organize

- Write a description of your perfect world. (*Example: My perfect world is a place where all people know God through a personal relationship with Jesus Christ and live according to God's mission for their lives.*)

_____

_____

_____

_____

- From the previous two activities, combine two of your nouns and two of your verbs with your definition of a perfect world. This will be the foundation for your life mission statement.

_____

_____

_____

_____

The nouns Ken picked were *teacher* and *example*. The verbs were *help* and *motivate*. His picture of the world is *everyone would have the presence of God in their lives*. As a result, Ken's mission statement is *To be a loving teacher and example of simple truths that helps myself and others awaken the presence of God in our lives.*

Your Personal Picture of the Future

Your picture of the future suggests what your life would look like if you were living "on purpose" all the time. The way Ken developed his picture of the future was by writing his own obituary. That might seem morbid, but it actually is a beneficial exercise. Ken became interested in his own obituary when he read about Alfred Nobel. When Alfred's brother died, the newspaper confused Alfred's life with his brother's life. Therefore, while drinking coffee one morning, Alfred Nobel was able to read his own obituary. Nobel could not believe that he would be remembered for the destruction and devastation associated with his most famous invention—dynamite. Nobel refocused his life so that he would not be remembered for destruction, but for peace. Thus, the Nobel Peace Prize came into existence.

Spend some time writing the obituary you would like to have published upon your death in the space below.

_____

_____

_____

_____

_____

Your Personal Values

Your values are what you stand for. They drive your behavior. In developing your personal values, remember three things:

1. Don't have too many values. Three to five are the most you can handle if you expect your values to guide your behavior.

2. Prioritize your values. Life is about values conflicts. Sometimes you have to choose between your values. As a result, they need to be rank-ordered.

3. Your values have to have behavioral indicators. How will you know when you are living according to a value?

After you have edited and refined your mission statement and your obituary, begin to identify your values in the spaces below.

I value _____ and I know that I am living by that value when _____ _____.

I value _____ and I know that I am living by that value when _____ _____.

I value _____ and I know that I am living by that value when _____ _____.

I value _____ and I know that I am living by that value when _____ _____.

Now refine your values statement and be prepared to discuss today's activities in the next small group meeting.

_____

_____

_____

 ## Key Concepts

As we develop our own values priorities, it is important to know and understand what Jesus set before us as His nonnegotiable priorities. When the Pharisees sought to test Jesus with the question, "Teacher, which is the greatest commandment in the Law?" Jesus replied, "Love the Lord your God with all your heart and with all your soul and with all your mind. This is the first and greatest commandment. And the second is like it: 'Love your neighbor as yourself.' All the Law and the Prophets hang on these two commandments." (Matt. 22:36–40)

Notice that Jesus rank-ordered two values:

1. Love God with all your heart, soul, and mind.

2. Love your neighbor as yourself.

As His followers and disciples follow His way of leading, we are called to make His values our leadership values and His priorities our priorities. Even if they are rank-ordered, values will not drive the accomplishment of a purpose or picture of the future unless they are translated into behaviors.

That's what Jesus did throughout his three-year public ministry. Clarifying how values are lived out in behavioral terms allows for accountability and measurement of progress.

 ## A Point to Ponder

Imagine you were being interviewed by your ten-year-old daughter and she asked you, "What are the four most important rules in our family and which one comes first?" What would your answer be?

▶ Next Steps

Write the mission statement you developed this week in the space provided below, and circle the action words that appear in your statement. What step(s) will you take today to begin implementing your mission statement?

_____

_____

_____

_____

_____

_____

DEVELOPING A COMPELLING VISION FOR YOUR ORGANIZATION OR YOUR FAMILY

Quote for Today

If your vision is for a year, plant wheat. If your vision is for ten years, plant trees. If your vision is for a lifetime, plant people.[5]

Chinese Proverb

What God's Word Says

Whatever you do, work at it with all your heart, as working for the Lord, not for men, since you know that you will receive an inheritance from the Lord as a reward. It is the Lord Christ you are serving. (Col. 3:23–24)

Pause and Reflect

What does the passage above say your attitude toward your leadership responsibilities should be?

_____

_____

_____

_____

_____

_____

A Prayer for Today:

Lord, I give you my heart, I give You my all, and I live for You alone. Every breath that I take, every moment I'm awake, I live for You alone. Make my vision Your vision, and may I live it to the fullest every day! In Jesus's Name, Amen!

Today's Topic
DEVELOPING A COMPELLING VISION FOR YOUR ORGANIZATION OR YOUR FAMILY

It really doesn't matter what you are doing, you are supposed to do it as if you are serving the Lord. That means leadership should emulate Jesus's example. How many times have you heard about Christians who seemed to abandon their faith for the purposes of reaching their professional goals?

Learning to lead like Jesus sometimes involves working inside a larger organization where we are not in the position to define the overall purpose, values, and picture of the future. Even in such circumstances we have a responsibility to meet the needs of those in our care in a way that is compatible with the servant leader mandate we have from Jesus.

• Write A for agree or D for disagree for the following statements:

_____ In an organization without vision, activity is expected but progress is optional.

_____ Without a sense of purpose, a life is spent but not invested.

_____ A river without banks is just a large puddle.

_____ If you accomplish your mission it doesn't matter what happens to the people.

One of the reasons organizations are bureaucratic is because no one knows what the organization does, where it's going, or who should guide its journey. The same can be said for families where competing individual agendas and points of view create frenzy and chaos.

• Write your organization's purpose, picture of the future, and values. You may choose your business, your church, your family, or your group as your organization.

• What is your organizational purpose/mission?

_____

_____

• What is your organizational view of the future that can excite your people?

_____

_____

• What operating values can your customers/clients depend on to guide your organization?

_____

_____

_____

Your Organizational Purpose

What's the point of your organization? What are you trying to accomplish? What would be missing if your organization no longer existed? What is your mission statement? Jesus called His disciples not to just become fishermen, but to a greater purpose—to become *fishers of men* (Matthew 4:19). It is one thing to have a self-centered focus—fishing. It is another thing to take that focus and redirect it to God's purposes—fishers of men.

An effective mission statement should express a higher purpose for the greater good that gives meaning to the efforts of each individual involved in your organization. If everyone does not understand your purpose or is not excited and passionate about it, your organization will begin to lose its way.

Creating a Clear Purpose

When Walt Disney started his theme parks, he knew how to excite people. He said, "We are in the happiness business—we make magic!" That clear purpose drives everything the cast members—or employees—do with their guests.

If an organization's stated mission does not support a higher purpose, it will not motivate people. For instance, a congregation said they wanted to be a twenty-four-hour-a-day church. The idea was that they wanted their facility to be used around the clock. However, attendance decreased because the mission didn't elicit excitement. Your purpose needs to excite people. It must inspire people to forget about themselves and join together for a higher purpose.

In 1999, upon the founding of the Center for Faithwalk Leadership (now known as Lead Like Jesus), we experimented with several different purpose statements. While our early drafts were helpful in explaining our general purpose, they weren't very inspiring. Our task—to help leaders move from success to significance by adopting the concepts of servant leadership—was easy to grasp. However, expressing it in an inspirational way was a challenge.

In 2002, with the help of the Brandtrust organization, we finalized our purpose statement: *To challenge and equip people to Lead Like Jesus.* The impact was immediate and powerful. We got excited, our staff got excited, our national board got excited, and our customers got excited. We are pretty sure God was pleased, too. In 2003, it was changed again to read *To inspire and equip people to Lead Like Jesus.*

If your organization does not have a purpose/mission statement or if it is not clearly stated, try to restate it. Laurie Beth Jones says a mission statement has three elements.[5]

1. A mission statement should be no more than one sentence long.

2. A mission statement should be easily understood by a twelve-year-old.

3. A mission statement should be able to be recited from memory at gunpoint.

• Write or rewrite your organization's purpose/mission statement below using the criteria above.

_____

_____

Your Organizational or Family Picture of the Future

The second element of a compelling vision is your picture of the future. You must ask yourself, "What will the future look like if things are running as planned?" Jesus outlined this for His disciples when He charged them, "Therefore, go and make disciples of all nations, baptizing them in the name of the Father and of the Son and of the Holy Spirit, and teaching them to obey everything I have commanded you. And surely I am with you always, to the very end of the age" (Matt. 28:19–20).

That was His picture of the future. At Lead Like Jesus, our picture of the future is, *we want to establish the Lead Like Jesus movement everywhere, so someday everyone knows someone who truly leads like Jesus.* To accomplish that we envision the following:

1. Jesus is adopted as the role model for all leaders.
2. All people are drawn to Jesus by the positive impact of Christians leading like Jesus.

Look Inside

Your picture of the future assumes you are living according to your purpose and values.

• What is your picture of the future? What uncertainties do you have regarding your picture of the future?

_____

_____

• What does a good job look like?

_____

_____

• What will the future look like if things are going as planned?

_____

_____

Providing detailed answers to these questions is important in guiding the long-range results and relationships of both organizations and families.

The view of the future is what keeps people going when things get tough. It prevents them from stopping short or from arriving at the wrong destination. In your view of the future it is important to distinguish between *goals* and *vision*. A goal is a specific event that once achieved becomes a piece of history to be superseded by a new goal. A vision or *view of the future* is an ongoing, evolving, hopeful look into the future that stirs the hearts and minds of people who know they will never see its end or its limit.

Throughout His ministry Jesus spoke of what His kingdom looked like. He continually talked about the kingdom—its values, teachings, parables, miracles, and final fulfillment. He gave the disciples a clear picture of the future and they committed themselves to it.

Look Inside:

- What are the pictures of the future for your organization and your family?

  Organization: _____

  Family: _____

- What are your roles in helping your organization and your family move toward that vision?

  Organization: _____

  Family: _____

- How does your relationship with God affect your participation in your organization's and your family's visions?

  Organization: _____

  Family: _____

Key Concepts

- Leadership is about going somewhere. Effective leadership begins with a clear vision, whether for your personal life, your family, or an organization.

- If your followers don't know where you are going and where you are trying to take them, they will have a hard time getting excited about the journey.

- No organization or cause will rise beyond the passion and the purpose of the leader. If you are not committed to a preferred view of the future for those you lead then you are engaging in an exercise in hypocrisy and wrongful use of your influence.

- Jesus calls us to follow Him in the highest calling—to glorify God and love one another where He has already demonstrated His passion unto death.

A Point to Ponder

A vision without action is called a daydream; but then again, action without a vision is called a nightmare.

- Jim Sorensen

▶ Next Steps

As a follower of Jesus, what is a word or phrase that describes your vision for your future?

_____

_____

_____

For your family's future?

_____

_____

_____

For the future of your organization?

_____

_____

_____

What next step(s) can you take to make these visions reality?

_____

_____

_____

THE ROLE OF VALUES IN *LEADING LIKE JESUS*

 ### Quote for Today

The ultimate determinant in the struggle now going on for the world will not be bombs and rockets, but a test of wills and ideas—a trial of spiritual resolve; the values we hold, the beliefs we cherish, and the ideals to which we are dedicated.[6]

Ronald Reagan

 ### What God's Word Says

Show me your faith without deeds, and I will show you my faith by what I do. You believe that there is one God. Good! Even the demons believe that—and shudder. (James 2:18b–19)

What governs the way you behave? James argued that it is impossible to have an authentic relationship with God and your behavior not be changed. This is when God's values become your values.

 ### Pause and Reflect

• What is the relationship between what you believe and your leadership style?

_____ My leadership style and my religious beliefs should be kept separate.

_____ My faith determines my leadership style.

_____ My leadership style determines my faith.

_____ I should not limit my leadership style to the boundaries of my faith.

 ### A Prayer for Today

Lord, You clearly presented Your values to us as You walked on the earth. Of course, they were given thousands of years ago. I realize that I am driven by values every today—the choices I make each day are based on a set of written and unwritten values. I choose today to make my choices based on Your values. I want them written on my heart so that, at a moment's notice, I will choose wisely and best. In Jesus's Name, Amen!

Today's Topic
THE ROLE OF VALUES IN *LEADING LIKE JESUS*

The third element of a compelling vision is values. Values are the nonnegotiable principles that define character in a leader, an organization, and a family. Fewer than ten percent of organizations around the world have clear, written values.

The number of families who have something similar written down is miniscule but they are lived out in what is accepted in behavior and attitudes. The impact of values on both results and relationships are important, because they frame people's behavior while they are engaged in implementing your purpose and picture of the future.

Research shows that if you really want to impact behavior you can't emphasize more than three or four values, because people can't focus on more than that. Why is it important to state and prioritize your values? Because life is about values conflicts! When these conflicts arise, people need to know what values should guide their responses. Walt Disney seemed to sense both of these things when he prioritized and rank-ordered his organization's operating values.

Below are listed the four values Disney established for his theme parks. Rank them in order you think Disney would have ranked them from 1 (the highest priority) to 4 (the lowest):

_____ Courtesy

_____ The Show

_____ Efficiency

_____ Safety

When most people think about Disney, they list courtesy as the first value followed by efficiency. They put safety third and the show fourth. However, for Disney, safety was his first priority. Disney knew that if guests left the park in an ambulance, they probably would not be leaving with the same smile they had when they arrived!

The fact that your values must be rank-ordered is important, because life is all about value choices. Unless a leader defines what takes priority, it will be left up to individuals to create their own priorities. When that happens, an organization or a family steers away from fulfilling their desired purpose and picture of the future. As we develop our own priorities it is important to know and to understand what Jesus set before us as His nonnegotiables.

When the Pharisees sought to test Jesus with the question, "Teacher, what is the greatest commandment in the Law?" Jesus replied, "Love the Lord your God with all your heart and with all your soul and with all your mind. This is the first and greatest commandment. And the second is like it: 'Love your neighbor as yourself.' All the Law and the Prophets hang on these two commandments." (Matt. 22:36–40)

Jesus rank-ordered His values:

1. Love God with all your heart, soul, and mind.

2. Love your neighbor as yourself.

 ## Look Inside

What are your values? What do you stand for? What are the nonnegotiables of your organization and your family?

- Write in your own words the key values of your organization and your family. Rank them in order of preference.

Family:

1.

2.

3.

4.

Organization:

1.

2.

3.

4.

Now prayerfully consider and take as much time as you need to answer the following question: Do the values and priorities of your organization and your family line up with those that Jesus calls all of his followers to adopt for their lives and relationships?

Family:_____

_____

_____

Organization: _____

_____

_____

If they do, praise God and keep your eyes on Jesus. If they don't, ask God to show you how to bring them into harmony with His will. Then proceed accordingly.

Where the Proof is Found

Unless values are translated into behaviors, they will not drive the accomplishment of a purpose or a picture of the future. Clarifying how values are lived out in behavioral terms allows for accountability and measurement of progress.

At Lead Like Jesus our values priorities and the behaviors they signal are as follows:

Homor God in everything we do.

We will know we are living by this value when we . . .

- Give God all the credit
- Relinquish all problems to His care
- Seek His face through:

    Worshiping together

    Studying together

    Praying together

- Love one another as He loves us by:

    Being a loving truth-teller

    Honoring each other's commitments

    Encouraging each other's health and well-being

    Proceed by boldly living the message

Maintain integrity and excellence in programs and services.

We will know we are living by this value when we . . .

- Filter every action through our purpose statement
- Use the Bible, with reference, as our primary source for guidance in the development of all materials and services
- Engage the best thinkers and practitioners of Jesus-like leadership
- Seek and honor feedback from all stakeholders for continuous improvement
- Speak the truth and deal honestly in all our relationships

Build relationships based on trust and respect.

We will know we are living by this value when we . . .

- Trust each other
- Seek each other's counsel and involvement in decision making
- Support one another on goal accomplishment
- Engage in unfiltered conflict around ideas
- Commit to decisions and plans of action
- Hold each other accountable for those plans
- Focus on achievement for collective results
- Practice openness and vulnerability
- Use mistakes as opportunities to learn rather than punish

Practice sound stewardship.

We will know we are living by this value when we . . .

- Share financial statements with all stakeholders
- Budget and expand resources wisely based on our purpose and commitment to stakeholders
- Respond gratefully to our contributors
- Ensure our alliances and funding sources are committed to and compatible with our purpose
- Implement sound financial and auditing practices
- Maintain a balance between serving customers and financial responsibility
- Implement effective use of time, talent, and resources

Making Tough Values Choices

Many of us will be or already are working in organizations and institutions that have established, even by default, a set of operating values. The fact that conflicts between organizational values and personal values will occur is a reality of life. What do you do when the values of the organization do not align with your own? You may realize this over time as you experience ongoing gaps between formal statements of policy and purpose and what is acted out on a daily basis. You are faced with a choice between rationalizing a compromise to your values, seeking to be an active influence for change in the organization, or leaving the organization.

Leading like Jesus does not include letting the organization change your values. The core of the temptation to compromise your own values is likely to stem from EGO issues—particularly toxic fears such as the fear of rejection, fear of failure, fear of poverty, fear of ridicule, fear of confrontation, or fear of lost position.

Jesus dealt with this problem of choice when He spoke of the impossibility of serving two masters at the same time.

> "No servant can serve two masters. Either he will hate the one and love the other, or he will be devoted to the one and despise the other. You cannot serve both God and money" (Luke 16:13).

He posed the ultimate challenge to compromise by spelling out the long-range price when He said, "What good is it for a man to gain the whole world, and yet lose or forfeit his very self?" (Luke 9:25).

He also told us that we can trust in His promise never to leave us alone or outside the range of His care and concern for us.

Leading like Jesus does include the possibility of making a choice either to be an agent of change or to seek a more compatible environment. The appropriate response for your circumstance will depend on what God has in mind for you.

Life is all about choices. Choices are made based on your values, whether you admit it or not. You are a monument to the choices you have made over the course of your life. If you want to change your life, embrace the values of Christ, the servant leader.

Look Inside

• Are you facing a values conflict within your organization? If so, consider your options in light of what you learned in today's reading.

STAY because . . .

_____

LEAVE because . . .

_____

Pray that God will show you your values and the choices He wants you to make based on those values.

Key Concepts

• Values are the nonnegotiable principles modeled by a leader, and they reflect the highest standards others can be called to serve.

• Values need to be ranked to give followers the best chance of serving the long range vision in dealing with daily value conflicts and choices

A Point to Ponder

In John 21:15–18, before Jesus restored Peter to a leadership role, He asked him only one qualifying question—_Do you love me?_ When in doubt do you do the loving thing?

Next Steps

Life is about choices! What is one choice that you have made that causes you to celebrate?

_____

What is one that causes you sadness?

_____

What can you learn about values from these two experiences?

_____

_____

VISION AND IMPLEMENTATION

 Quote for Today

We either love people or we control them. There's little room for anything else. And it's far easier to control them than to love them.[7]

John Eldredge

 What God's Word Says

Love must be sincere. Hate what is evil; cling to what is good. Be devoted to one another in brotherly love. Honor one another above yourselves. (Rom. 12:9–10)

⏸ Pause and Reflect

Plot your leadership style on the continuum below by placing an **X** on the line.

I control people _____ I love people

Paul's words challenge us to value others above ourselves. Why is that so difficult to do?

_____

_____

_____

_____

_____

 A Prayer for the Day

Lord, Your Word is full of opportunities for me to demonstrate Your character to the world around me. As I read through the Bible, help me to see, learn, and practice those truths that will change me and others, as they see them lived out in my life. In Jesus's Name, Amen!

Today's Topic
VISION AND IMPLEMENTATION

The traditional pyramidal hierarchy is effective for the first role of leadership—the *vision-ary* role. People look to the leader for vision and direction. While the leader should involve experienced people in shaping direction, the ultimate responsibility remains with the leader and cannot be delegated to others. In the diagram below, the leader is responsible and the followers are responsive. The pyramid illustrates the concepts we've been discussing so far this week.

Implementing a Clear Vision

Now we must turn the pyramid upside down for the second role of leadership—the *implemen-tation* of the vision. The people who have the primary contact with the public must be on top and the leader on the bottom supporting them. The implementation phase looks like this:

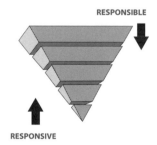

The *implementation* role of leaders—living according to the vision and direction you have set—is where most leaders and organizations get into trouble. The traditional hierarchical pyramid is kept alive so that all the energy is moving away from the customers, up the hier-archies, because people feel they must please their bosses, leaving the customers neglected at the bottom of the hierarchy. This happens a lot in organizations. In this environment, self-serving leaders assume the sheep are there for the benefit of the shepherd. Jesus was talking against this kind of authoritarian hierarchy when He said, "not so with you" (Matt. 20:26).

If you don't turn the pyramid upside down, you have a duck pond. When there is a conflict between what the customers want and what the boss wants, the boss wins. You have people quacking like ducks: "It's our policy." "I just work here." "Would you like me to get my supervisor?" A *Lead Like Jesus* leader doesn't want that! Servant leadership will be most evident in your behavior during the implementation phase of your vision In this stage, your job is to be responsive to the needs of the people serving the vision and to your customers. To do this you have to get your ego out of the way. When Jesus washed the feet of His disciples, He was transitioning His focus from the visionary/direction part of leadership to the implementation role. As He did that, He was turning the pyramid upside down. He was not implying that the disciples should go out and help people do anything they wanted. The vision was clear. He got it from the top of the hierarchy—His Father.

As *fishers of men* they were *to go make disciples of all nations,* focusing first on loving God and then on loving their neighbors. But when it came to implementing this vision, Jesus wanted His disciples to be servant leaders. He said the least shall be the greatest, the last shall be first, and the one who would be great would be the servant.

Horst Schulze helped create the Ritz Carlton—one of the greatest service organizations in the United States. Horst believed in turning the pyramid upside down, so that every frontline employee had $2,000 in discretionary funds they could use to solve customer problems without consulting anyone. That is putting people into positions where they can soar like eagles.

Serving the Vision

Jesus was precise about the vision for His ministry. He was clear about the final exam. Once your vision is clear and the final exam is determined, then you as the leader are to initiate the day-to-day coaching. You prepare people to be able to pass the final exam, to live according to the vision. It is the vision—the purpose, picture of the future, and values—that everyone should serve.

Jesus said, ". . . the Son of Man did not come to be served, but to serve" (Matt. 20:28). What did He come to serve? He came to serve the vision He had been given by His Father. He came as a teacher, as a leader, as a trainer to prepare people to go out and help other people live according to that vision. To do so, He served people.

As servant leaders, we are not asked to die for our people. However, Jesus's model of leadership still reminds us that His way is not the world's way. Servant leadership Jesus's way starts with a vision and ends with a servant heart that helps people live according to the vision.

Leading People Like Jesus Did

When we put the *heart* and the *head* together in a *Lead Like Jesus* perspective, people come to the forefront and self takes the back seat. How do you serve people in a way that reflects Jesus's point of view? Jesus's prayer on the last night of His ministry (John 17) gives us some guidelines. Jesus knew His people intimately, He respected them profoundly, and He equipped them to be competent and confident leaders.

Equipping Others by Sharing Vital Information and Insuring Understanding of the Situation

Read John 17:6–8 and identify how Jesus equipped others by sharing information and being sure His followers understood the situation.

> I have revealed you to those whom you gave me out of the world. They were yours; you gave them to me and they have obeyed your word. Now they know that everything you have given me comes from you. For I gave them the words you gave me and they accepted them. They knew with certainty that I came from you, and they believed you sent me.

• Jesus equipped others by:

_____

_____

_____

In today's world, almost everyone can access the same information the leader can. The issue now is one of willingness to share information rather than logistics of sharing it. Practicing open communication and keeping people informed serves as the implementation of the vision by building trust and commitment. Ego-driven leaders who are afraid of losing control or who are insecure in their positions tend to hoard information rather than share it.

Providing Protection and Coaching Future Leaders

• Read John 17:12.

> "While I was with them, I protected them and kept them safe by that name you gave me."

How did Jesus protect and equip His future leaders?

_____

_____

_____

Jesus continued to support and interact with the disciples as they grew in competence and commitment. He provided a safe harbor where they could grow in understanding as thy practiced right behavior and as their competence and commitment were developed, although imperfectly. He stayed with His followers until it was time for them to go out on their own, and even then He followed up with them.

Relinquishing Control to Facilitate Growth and Development

• Read John 17:11 and John 16:7.

> "I will remain in the world no longer, but they are still in the world and I am coming to You" (John 17:11).

"Now I am going to him who sent me . . . It is for your good that I am going away. Unless I go away, the Counselor will not come to you; but if I go, I will send him to you" (John 16:5a, 7).

What did Jesus do to facilitate the spiritual growth of His followers?

_____

_____

Knowing when to delegate is the fine art of servant leadership. Premature delegation isn't empowerment, it is abdication of responsibility. Continuing to micromanage once you have delegated prevents experimentation and growth. Jesus knew that none of His disciples could step to the front as leaders like He intended for them to do as long as He was with them. He often warned them that He would be crucified and that they would take up His mission. Only when He left them were they able to do it. However, He did not leave them alone. He promised ". . . surely I am with you always, to the very end of the age" (Matt. 28:20).

Making Provisions for the Future Well-being of Those on the Vision

• Read John 17:13-18.

> I am coming to you now, but I say these things while I am still in the world, so that they may have full measure of my joy within them. I have given them your word and the world has hated them, for they are not of the world any more than I am of the world. My prayer is not that you take them out of the world but that you protect them from the evil one. They are not of the world, even as I am not of it. Sanctify them by the truth; your word in truth. As you sent me into the world, I have sent them to the world. For them I sanctify myself, that they too may be truly sanctified.

How did Jesus make provisions for the future well-being of His followers?

_____

_____

_____

Jesus's prayer shows His deep concern for the future of His disciples. He provided them the full measure of His joy within them. He gave them the Father's Word. He prayed for their protection. He asked the Father to sanctify them as He was. He sent them into the world prepared. He gave them everything they needed, although it was not everything they wanted at the beginning. He promised them,

> ". . . no one who has left home or wife or brothers or parents of children for the sake of the kingdom of God will fail to receive many times as much in this age and, in the age to come, eternal life" (Luke 18:29–30).

As a leader you must do all you can to ensure the well-being of those who are working with you. There is no higher calling for a leader whose followers have entrusted their days, years, and lives to his care than to lay down his life for them.

Look Inside

In summary, remember that servant leadership, as it relates to the *head* (leadership assumptions and methods) involves seven things. Check all the statements you intend to practice:

_____ 1. Reflect the highest purpose and vision you personally have been called to serve as the foundation for the purpose and vision you call other people to serve

_____ 2. Communicate a compelling picture of what a preferred view of the future will look like if all who are committed to its coming true seek to serve the vision and one another

_____ 3. Define and model the operating values, structure, and behavior that you are willing to be held accountable to model and that you want from those you lead

_____ 4. Create an environment of mutual service and empowerment

_____ 5. Move to the bottom of the pyramid to support those who are now responsible to serve

_____ 6. Model the highest respect for everyone

_____ 7. Make the growth, development, and respect of people an end goal of equal importance with the attainment of performance results

Jesus did all these things. He was really clear with people about why He came, what the good news was, and what He wanted people to do. Then He modeled implementing servant leadership with everyone He met.

Key Concepts

- Servant Leadership involves:
  - Setting the vision
  - Defining and modeling the operating values, structure, and behavioral norms
  - Creating the follower environment with partners in the vision
  - Moving to the bottom of the hierarchy with service in mind

A Point to Ponder

Servant leadership requires a level of intimacy with the needs and aspirations of the people being led, which might be beyond the level of intimacy an ego-driven leader is willing to sustain.

Next Steps

". . . Go and do likewise" (Luke 10:37).

week four

4

THE *HANDS* OF A SERVANT LEADER, PART 1

Memory Verse for the Week

"Come follow me," Jesus said, "
and I will make you fishers of men"
(Matt. 4:19).

How do you want your leadership to be remembered by the people at work, at home, in your church, and in your community? Leading like Jesus is not a course, it is a lifestyle! Making the development of people an equal partner with performance is a decision you make. It is following the example of Jesus as a servant leader and pouring your life into the lives of other people. It is about leaving a leadership legacy of service.

Leading like Jesus is more than a theory or a hopeful sentiment. It is a call to obedience in leadership as an expression of who you are following: Jesus. It means actually changing your behavior to be more like Jesus and starting to ask "What would Jesus do?" before you act.

This week you will evaluate your actions as a leader and how you need to vary your leadership style based on the needs of the people you are leading. You will see from Scripture how Jesus varied His leadership style so that He could meet the needs of those He encountered daily (the disciples) and those with whom He had brief, but life-changing encounters.

4 week four

PERFORMANCE COACHING

❝❞ Quote for Today

When Jesus called His disciples to follow Him, He pledged them His full support and guidance as they developed into "fishers of men." This is the duty of a servant leader—the ongoing investment of the leader's life into the lives of those who follow.[1]

Ken Blanchard and Phil Hodges

📖 What God's Word Says

As Jesus was walking beside the Sea of Galilee, he saw two brothers, Simon called Peter and his brother Andrew. They were casting a net into the lake, for they were fishermen. "Come, follow me," Jesus said, "and I will make you fishers of men." At once they left their nets and followed him. Going on from there, he saw two other brothers, James son of Zebedee and his brother John. They were in a boat with their father, Zebedee, preparing their nets. Jesus called them, and immediately they left the boat and their father and followed him. (Matt. 4:18–22)

⏸ Pause and Reflect

Reconsider the passage above in relationship to your position of leadership. Describe how Jesus called you and the purpose for which you were called.

_____

_____

_____

🖐 A Prayer for Today

Lord, just as You called the disciples of old, so You call disciples today. While I may not have fishing nets to leave, the call is the same. Thank You that You don't call me because I'm qualified, but because You will qualify me for the task You have prepared for me before the foundation of the world. In Jesus's Name, Amen!

Today's Topic
PERFORMANCE COACHING

Jesus didn't tell Simon Peter, Andrew, James, and John that He would give them a self-study course, send them to a seminar, or provide them with an education at a prestigious university. He said, "I will make you . . ." This is an important distinction in the life of the servant leader. Servant leaders are shepherds, not herdsmen. Shepherds lead with love and nurture. Herdsmen lead with force and fear. Jesus redefined leadership in a way that rocked the world then and continues to rock the world now.

A key activity of an effective servant leader is to act as a performance coach. When Jesus called His disciples to follow Him, He pledged to them His full support and guidance as they developed into *fishers of men*. This is the duty of a servant leader—the ongoing investment of the leader's life into the lives of those who follow. By being a performance coach and changing his leadership style appropriately as His disciples developed individually and as a group, Jesus empowered His followers to carry on after He was gone. Through His *hands* (effective leadership behavior), He was able to transmit what was in His *heart* and *head* about servant leadership.

The Servant Leader as a Performance Coach

There are three parts to becoming a performance coach: performance planning, day-to-day coaching, and performance evaluation.

- Before we begin, write in the space below your best guess as to what each of the following parts of being a performance coach involves:

Performance planning:

_____

_____

Day-to-day coaching:

_____

_____

Performance evaluation:

_____

_____

As you read the following descriptions, evaluate your answers.

Performance planning is you setting the goals. Remember, all good performance starts with clear goals. College professors generally distribute syllabi to their students in order to clearly communicate the goals for the course. The goals provide not only the requirements but also the criteria by which the achievement of the goals will be measured.

Day-to-day coaching involves observing people's performance, praising progress, and redirecting efforts that are off base. Many leaders avoid this process because it is labor and time intensive.

Performance evaluation is a look back at someone's effort to achieve a goal. In an academic environment, students are given final exams or final projects. Professors are subjected to evaluations by their students—this is the professor's final exam.

Which of these three activities—performance planning, day-to-day coaching, or performance evaluation—do you think gets the most attention and effort by leaders in organizations? Rank the tasks in order of priority (with 3 being lowest and 1 being highest):

_____ performance planning

_____ day-to-day coaching

_____ performance evaluation

Most people guess performance evaluation and, unfortunately, that is the truth. When we visit organization after organization and ask about their performance review system, they show us their evaluation forms. We usually tell them they can throw most of the forms out. Why? Because those forms usually measure things like *willingness to take responsibility*, *initiative*, *promotability*, which are very difficult to judge in an objective way! As a result, everyone is trying to figure out how to please the boss on their own. The traditional top-down hierarchy is alive and well.

When it comes to *performance planning*, it is the leaders' responsibility at all levels to represent the organizational goals and provide guidance in developing the individual goals of their members.

When Moses went to the top of the mountain to get the Ten Commandments, he didn't take a committee with him. Otherwise, he would have come down with three commandments and seven suggestions. Jesus didn't often involve His disciples in the goals He came to accomplish. He got those from the top of the hierarchy—from His Father.

That does not mean that in our work in the home, community, and office we shouldn't involve others in goal setting. It does mean, though, that the impetus for clear goal setting has to come from the servant leader.

We can't emphasize enough the importance of clarity of purpose in the planning for the performance role of a servant leader. If there is not clear communication of what a good job will look like when it is accomplished, somebody will end up frustrated—either the leader or the follower, or both.

Think back to a time when you were on either side of a failure in communications. What was expected and what was delivered? Recall the frustration and wasted energy that could have been avoided by testing for understanding. When the leader isn't clear on exactly what *they* are looking for, or leave too much to the follower's imagination, the results will always be uncertain.

Look Inside

- Review each of the following goals and rate the chances of a *well done* being given when the task was completed.

Goal	Chances of a Well Done		
	Poor	Fair	Excellent
Do your best not to upset the customer.			
Clean up your room.			
Improve employee satisfaction by Tuesday.			
Bring me a rock.			
Support the growth of small groups in the church.			

- What could a leader do to improve the chances of a follower receiving a *well done*?

  _____

  _____

  _____

- How could the follower improve the chances of receiving a *well done*?

  _____

  _____

  _____

Key Concepts

- Three elements of day-to-day leadership are essential to attaining the results and relationships of servant leadership: Performance planning, day-to-day performance coaching, and performance evaluation.

- If there is not clear communication of what a good job will look like when it is accomplished, somebody will end up frustrated—either the leader or the follower or both.

- The biggest test of a leader's commitment to the success of his vision will be his level of willingness to invest his own efforts in day-to-day coaching and reinforcement of values.

A Point to Ponder

Often leaders limit the goal-setting portion of their leadership to proclaiming something they have in their mind's eye and then holding their people accountable for not being clairvoyant.

Think about someone in your life who has invested time helping you succeed.

List a few things that person did and how you were coached into achieving your goals.

_____

_____

_____

_____

_____

_____

What can you do to help someone get A's on her final exam? For the answer to that question, we can study how Jesus moved from a Carpenter to a Servant Leader who had a practical day-to-day coaching model for growing and developing people.

▶ Next Steps

Who needs to receive performance coaching from you right now? How will you begin to help them?

_____

_____

_____

_____

From whom do you need to receive performance coaching?

_____

_____

week four

THE LEADERSHIP JOURNEY FROM CALLED TO COMMISSIONED

Quote for Today

God doesn't call people who are qualified. He calls people who are willing, and then qualifies them.[2]

Richard Parker

What God's Word Says

". . . go and make disciples of all nations, baptizing them in the name of the Father and of the Son and of the Holy Spirit, and teaching them to obey everything I have commanded you. And surely I will be with you always even to the very end of the age" (Matt. 28:19–20).

Pause and Reflect

A faith relationship with Jesus Christ has a universal calling—go and make disciples. How are you fulfilling this responsibility in your daily tasks?

_____

_____

_____

_____

_____

A Prayer for Today

Lord, I am called to be a disciple and a disciple-maker. While both tasks seem daunting, I know that you have perfectly equipped me to be me and to reach those You send my way. I want to partner with You, knowing You will never leave me or forsake me. You are but a prayer away. So today may I be a faithful steward of the gift and the Giver. In Jesus's Name, Amen!

Today's Topic
THE LEADERSHIP JOURNEY FROM CALLED TO COMMISSIONED

When Jesus first called the disciples from their ordinary occupations to become *fishers of men*, each brought life experiences and skills to this new task but no practical knowledge of how to fulfill this new role. After spending three years under the leadership of Jesus, the disciples were transformed from untrained novices to fully-equipped, inspired, and spiritually-grounded leaders able to fulfill the Great Commission.

The people called to this new task came from various trades and professions and stations in society. Among those who He called were Matthew, the tax collector; Peter, the fisherman; Simon, the political activist; and later, Paul—one of the most educated men of his day—a rabbi, a lawyer, and also a tent-maker. What they did was less important than who they were and who they could be through the transforming power of God's grace.

Something happened on the way to Jerusalem. The three years were more than travel time, they were also training time. Jesus was fully aware both of His mission and the competence (or lack of competence) of His disciples. On more than one occasion, Jesus may have wondered if these ordinary people really could continue the mission after He was gone.

- Think about your role in the grand scheme of things. In what larger mission are you a key player?

  _____ I've never thought about a larger mission.

  _____ I'm not sure I want to be a part of a larger mission.

  _____ I'm willing, but scared about the larger mission.

  _____ I'm certain of the larger mission. It is _____.

In His three years with the disciples, Jesus had to move them from the point of recognizing His call to accepting His commission. It's a long way from *Come, follow Me* to *Go into all the world*.

How did Jesus go about accomplishing the transition from *called* to *commissioned*? Although miracles were involved, the process was not miraculous. It entailed the perfect execution of a very familiar process by a leader personally committed to accomplishing His goal through the growth and development of those who followed.

We believe the experience Jesus had as a learner, under instruction as a carpenter, provided Him with a practical model for growing and developing people. He was able to use this model to guide the learning experiences of His disciples. Having, presumably, been guided through four normal stages of learning a new task—novice, apprentice, journeyman, and master/teacher—Jesus brought to His season of leadership a clear understanding of what the journey from dependence to independence entailed.

Let's explore in more detail the four common terms for learning almost any new task or skill:

Novice—someone just starting out

Apprentice—someone in training

Journeyman—someone capable of working on his own

Master/teacher—someone highly skilled and able to teach others

The journey from novice to master/teacher is time-consuming. It can't be accomplished in a hurry. To progress from being a novice to becoming a master/teacher in any role or skill, learners need someone to provide them with supervision and encouragement along the way. *Novices* enter the learning process through an orientation phase and progress to a training phase as *Apprentices* until they gain sufficient command of the work to proceed on their own in an independent contributor phase. *Journeymen* develop the experience and advanced knowledge required to be endorsed and commissioned as *Master/Teachers*. The role of the leader is the same throughout the transformation process—to provide what the learner needs to advance to the next stage.

Look Inside

- In what area of your life are you in need of mentoring by a master/teacher?

  _____

  _____

- Who are the master/teachers God has brought into your life?

  _____

  _____

- Who are the people God has placed under your supervision for whom you can be a mentor?

  _____

  _____

- To what extent are you willing to be inconvenienced in order to give leadership to someone who is coming along behind you?

  _____

  _____

- To what extent are you willing to be inconvenienced in order to be mentored by someone who is ahead of you?

  _____

  _____

Key Concepts

- To progress from being a novice to becoming a master in any role or skill, learners need someone to guide them along the way and to give them what they need to advance through the learning process.

- The journey from novice to master/teacher is time-consuming. It can't be accomplished in a hurry and requires joint commitment between the leader and the follower that they will both devote what is needed to the process.

- When Jesus extended the invitation to the novice disciples to follow Him so He could make them into fishers of men, He committed Himself to their transformation with full knowledge of what it would cost.

- As a follower progresses through the learning process the leader has to be willing and able to alter their leadership style to provide the right combination of information and inspiration.

A Point to Ponder

Think about your relationship with God and your faith journey to date. You, too, are moving from being called to living out your commission. Place an X on the line representing where you are on the journey.

Called ————————————————|———————————— Living Out the Commission

- Explain your position in terms of your spiritual growth. What has contributed to your growth? What has hindered your growth?

  _____
  _____

- What are you actively doing to let Jesus mentor you on your journey?

  _____
  _____

Next Steps
A COMMITMENT TO THE PROCESS

Within the next week, I will actively seek out someone to mentor me along my journey to Lead Like Jesus. Within the next week, I will actively pray for an opportunity to mentor someone on their journey.

Date: _____ Signed: _____

4

THE NEEDS OF A NOVICE

Quote for Today

God asks no man whether he will accept life. That is not a choice. You must take it. The only choice is how.[3]

Henry Ward Beecher

What God's Word Says

But if serving the Lord seems undesirable to you, then choose for yourselves this day whom you will serve, whether the gods your forefathers served beyond the River, or the gods of the Amorites, in whose land you are living. But as for me and my household, we will serve the Lord. (Josh. 24:15)

⏸ Pause and Reflect

Rewrite the passage above stating the choice you must make each day. In what ways are you distracted from focusing on God?

_____

_____

_____

_____

_____

A Prayer for Today

Choices, choices, choices! Lord, every day is filled with choices. Sometime I choose rightly and You smile; sometimes I choose wrongly and You are disappointed but loving. Help me to be as gently kind to those I lead as You are to me. Give me the right words and right directions so that the novices under my care will sense Your love for them through me. In Jesus's Name, Amen!

Today's Topic
THE NEEDS OF A NOVICE

Novices are people who are just starting to perform a particular task or to accomplish an assigned goal. They need to know what, when, where, and how to do something. Novices need basic information before they can progress, and their mentor must provide that. Novices also need someone committed to their development to welcome them into the learning process. They need to feel that someone *in the know* thinks the work is important enough to invest time and energy to teach it correctly. The quickest way to turn off a novice is to delegate his orientation to someone who is bored and could care less about the success of the student.

When people begin a new task or goal as novices, they can be either excited about the opportunity or hesitant because they have been forced into an unwanted learning process. For example, a fifteen-year-old girl learning to drive a car will be excited, whereas a fifty-eight-year-old man learning to use a three-legged cane after suffering a stroke will probably be hesitant.

Both novices have to follow instructions that may be new or awkward. In the case of the teenager, her excitement at the thought of driving her friends to the beach after one or two lessons may cause her to be overconfident and prone to impatience with the learning process. In the case of the stroke victim, the *why* question may cause him to be reluctant to come to terms with the new reality in his life.

Look Inside

- Circle the needs of a novice in the section above.
- Recall the last "new" place you encountered. What were your basic needs?

_____

_____

_____

Jesus and the Novice Disciples

The disciples were certainly novices when Jesus first encountered them.

> As Jesus was walking beside the Sea of Galilee, he saw two brothers, Simon called Peter and his brother Andrew. They were casting a net into the lake, for they were fishermen. "Come, follow me," Jesus said "and I will make you fishers of men." At once they left their nets and followed him. (Matt. 4:18–20)

Jesus saw in these hardworking fishermen the raw material for the future leaders of the ministry He would leave in their care when His earthly season of leadership was completed. In their enthusiasm, they literally dropped what they were doing when He called them to the higher purpose of being fishers of men. Although they were enthusiastic, they had no idea of how to accomplish their new task. Remember, the task was to be *fishers of men*—not fishermen. Their learning stage was that of novices. At that stage of learning they were dependent on Jesus to teach them about the new task. Therefore to meet their learning needs, it was necessary for Jesus to focus on telling them what to do and how to do it. That's exactly what Jesus did when He sent the twelve disciples out for the first time to preach the Good News.

We believe that leaders in churches and in businesses often set people up for failure because they do not accept responsibility for recognizing and responding effectively to this orientation learning stage.

• Does your church or organization have in place a process for moving new leaders through the novice stage? How would you describe this process?

_____

_____

• What is the plan by which you move spiritual novices into deeper levels of spiritual understanding?

_____

_____

• Think about the people God has placed under your care and influence as novices. Which of the following statements best describes your leadership style with the novices God has entrusted to you?

_____ I make sure they get the basic information they need to begin and help them see how the task fits in to the vision and purpose we serve together.

_____ I compel them to shape up by using fear and by micromanaging.

_____ I delegate the orientation process to somebody else because I have more important things to do.

_____ I provide an exciting picture of the future—tell the people that they are great and then let them figure out the details on their own.

Key Concepts

• Novices need basic information before they can progress. Novices also need someone committed to their development to welcome them into the learning process. They need to feel that someone *in the know* thinks their work is important enough to invest time and energy to teach it right.

• When people begin a new task or goal as novices, they can be either excited about the opportunity or hesitant because they have been compelled into the learning process.

- The higher a novice's expectation is, the greater the challenge in guiding him or her through the let down that is bound to come when he or she finds that what they seek to learn is harder than originally thought.

A Point to Ponder

- If you were the only model of a leader seeking to lead like Jesus someone had to follow, what image of Jesus as a leader would they develop?

_____ They would see Jesus for exactly who He is.

_____ They might see Jesus in me on good days.

_____ I'm not so sure I know Jesus well enough to represent Him to anyone.

_____ They would see someone trying to altar their EGO and on a journey to lead like Jesus.

Next Steps

List the needs of a novice.

_____

_____

_____

_____

Think of a time when you were a novice and did not receive the information you needed, how did you feel? What was your experience? What could your mentor have done to make this better?

_____

_____

_____

_____

Think of a novice that you mentor. Does he or she receive what they need from you?

_____

_____

_____

_____

THE NEEDS OF AN APPRENTICE

Quote for Today
If you haven't learned to follow, you can't lead.[4]

Henrietta C. Mears

What God's Word Says
Timothy, my son, I give you this instruction in keeping with the prophecies once made about you, so that by following them you may fight the good fight, holding on to faith and a good conscience . . . (1 Tim. 1:18-19)

Pause and Reflect
• In what ways is a life of faith a fight? Describe the support system that sustains you through your spiritual struggles.

_____

_____

_____

_____

_____

A Prayer for Today
Lord, even as Timothy was a faithful follower of Paul and was eager to hear his instructions, so might I be even more eager to hear Your instructions for my life. As I lead others today, help me to remember what it was and is like to be a follower, for I follow You still. In Jesus's Name, Amen!

Today's Topic
THE NEEDS OF AN APPRENTICE

As someone in training, an *apprentice* has not yet mastered all the information and skills to work alone. Apprentices need verification that they are doing the right thing the right way, and they need to be corrected when they don't quite have it. They also need someone to help put their progress in the right perspective so they don't become overconfident with early success or discouraged with initial failure.

For example, the teenager learning to drive who has effectively fastened her seat belt and started the car on one of her practice runs begins to cry when she starts to pull out into traffic and is startled by a car racing by that she did not see. Her parent needs to praise her for fastening her seat belt and turning on the car correctly. She also needs to be quizzed on how the mirrors are to be adjusted and how she must look both ways to anticipate the flow of traffic.

The stroke victim learning to walk with a three-legged cane starts off well enough for a few steps, but then he becomes frustrated and angry because it takes him many minutes to travel a distance he could previously cover in seconds. The rehab nurse needs to praise him for what he has accomplished so far and put his rate of progress in perspective.

Look Inside

- Circle the needs of an apprentice in the section above.
- Recall the last time you were an apprentice. What did you need from your master/teacher? Did you get it? If not, what was the result?

_____

_____

Jesus and the Apprentice Disciples

Jesus had to respond to a number of situations with His disciples as they were apprenticing with Him. For example, the disciples quite possibly experienced one of those lows when they were unable to cast a demon out of a boy whose father had brought him to them. Casting out demons was one of the tasks Jesus assigned to them in Matthew 10 (vs. 1) when He sent them out. In Matthew 17:15–16 we read: "Lord, have mercy on my son," he said. "he has seizures and is suffering greatly. He often falls into the fire or into the water. I brought him to your disciples and they could not heal him."

When the disciples were new to the task of being fishers of men, they experienced a setback to their confidence as they discovered they were not competent to handle every situation. Think how the disciples must have felt when they were not able to succeed at casting out the demon. They must have been frustrated, uncertain and embarrassed.

Observe how Jesus responded to His disciples' disillusionment over not being able to cast out the demon. In Matthew 17:18–20 we read:

> Jesus rebuked the demon and it came out of the boy, and he was healed from that moment. Then the disciples came to Jesus in private and asked, "Why couldn't we drive it out?" He replied, "Because you have so little faith. I tell you the truth, if you have faith as small as a mustard seed, you can say to this mountain 'Move from here to there' and it will move. Nothing will be impossible for you.

Notice that in addressing the cause of their failure, Jesus gave the disciples truthful information as to why they were unable to cast out the demon—*because you have so little faith.*

Even when the disciples failed and He came behind them to *clean up their mess,* He still loved them and, we believe, expressed that love by telling them the truth in a loving way.

- How do you feel when you fail at a task you thought you could handle? (Check all that apply.)

_____ proud	_____ uncertain	_____ determined
_____ confused	_____ angry	_____ depressed
_____ embarrassed	_____ unconcerned	_____ happy

Your followers may experience those same feelings when confronted with a task or a goal they cannot do or in which they experienced a failure or problems. Sometimes the people you lead become discouraged about a specific task, while you as a leader are completely unaware of their disillusionment. If people become disillusioned and no one reaches out to them, they can become so discouraged that they give up and quit. Sometimes they will stay on the job but express their disillusionment by just going through the motions and negatively impact the enthusiasm and commitment of others.

Key Concepts

- Apprentices are people-in-training who have not yet mastered all the information and skills to work alone. They need to be assured that they are doing the right thing in the right way and to be corrected when they don't quite "have it." They also need someone to put their progress in the right perspective so they don't become overconfident with early success or discouraged with initial failure.

- Observation and speaking the truth with an intent to build on roughly right behavior and progress are key elements for serving the needs of an apprentice. It is vital to provide clear direction and information in a positive manner. If you are to follow the example of Jesus as a leader, never demean people or try to make them feel inferior because of a failure. Praise progress and redirect when needed to keep moving forward.

A Point to Ponder

Think of a time when you needed someone to push you beyond a failure or an easy early success to get to a higher level of understanding and performance in a new task. Think of a time when you quit because nobody was there to take you to the next level. Leading like Jesus requires perseverance. How are you regularly being spiritually strengthened?

_____

_____

_____

_____

It is vital that you provide clear direction and information to your apprentice, but that you do it in a loving manner. If you follow the example of Jesus, never demean people or try to make them feel small because of a failure on their part. As Jesus did, you should let the love you have for those with whom you work come through and let your desire to lead like Jesus always direct your behavior.

Next Steps

Give an example of someone you know who, as an apprentice, did not receive all of the information and training they needed. What was the result? What one thing could have made a difference in that person's life?

_____

_____

_____

_____

_____

THE NEEDS OF A JOURNEYMAN

 ## Quote for Today

It marks a big step in a man's development when he comes to realize that other men can be called in to help him do a better job than he can do alone.[5]

Andrew Carnegie

 ## What God's Word Says

What, after all, is Apollos? And what is Paul? Only servants, through whom you came to believe—as the Lord has assigned to each his task. I planted the seed, Apollos watered it, but God made it grow. (1 Cor. 3:5–6)

If anyone understood the value of teamwork, it was Paul. Paul progressed from novice to master/teacher, never forgetting the part others played in his ministry. We would do well to learn from Paul's example.

Pause and Reflect

Who are the other members of your leadership team and what are you doing to invest yourself in them?

_____

_____

_____

_____

 ## A Prayer for Today

Lord, thank You that You did not intend for me to work alone and that You've already prepared others to serve alongside me. Thanks for the Holy Spirit who also comes alongside to serve, guide, and direct. May I provide these same experiences for those I love and lead! In Jesus's Name, Amen!

Today's First Topic
THE NEEDS OF A JOURNEYMAN

It is easy to assume that someone who has acquired well-developed skills in performing a task or role has progressed to a point where all he or she needs from a leader is to be told when and where to apply those skills. The fact of the matter is that an experienced leader might periodically become cautious and lose confidence or enthusiasm for the job due to a variety of reasons. If left by inattentive leaders to quietly drift into apathy or retreat from taking risks, due to a feeling of lost competence or connection with their calling, journeymen can lose their skills and ability to perform. They will become disillusioned critics and skeptics who poison the attitudes of those who work around them. Leaders who ignore the journeymen's need for appreciation and encouragement do so at their peril.

Look Inside

- Circle the needs of a journeyman in the section above.

- Recall the last time you were a *Journeyman* at some task. What did you need from your master/teacher? Did you get it? If not, what was the result?

_____

_____

An example of a leader meeting the needs of a journeyman is a parent who hugs a teenage daughter after she becomes nervous and fails her first driving test, even though she received an A in drivers' education. Once she regains her composure, her parent encourages her to take the wheel and drive them home.

Another example is a rehab nurse who reminds the stroke victim of how far he has come in gaining his new skill and how proud of him she is as he prepares to use his cane in front of his family and friends.

Jesus and a Journeyman Disciple

Peter exhibited the behaviors characteristic of a journeyman when he walked on water. In Matthew 14:26-30 we read:

> When the disciples saw him walking on the lake, they were terrified. "It's a ghost," they said, and cried out in fear. But Jesus immediately said to them, "Take courage! It is I. Don't be afraid."
>
> "Lord, if it is you," Peter replied, "tell me to come to you on the water."
>
> "Come," He said. Then Peter got down out of the boat, walked on the water and came toward Jesus. But when he saw the wind, he was afraid and, beginning to sink, cried out, "Lord save me!"

Peter is a great illustration of someone capable of performing the task as he stepped on the water and began to walk! It took a tremendous amount of faith for Peter to step out of the boat and onto the water. So often we forget that Peter actually did walk on water! In fact, he was the only one besides Jesus who could list "walked on water" on his resume. Peter's problem, though, came when he took his eyes off of Jesus and began to worry about the storm. Peter's demonstrated competence sank into the water with him.

Jesus was there to provide the support that Peter needed when he started to sink, even after he had demonstrated the ability to walk on water. "Immediately Jesus reached out his hand and caught him. "You of little faith," he said, "why did you doubt?" And when they climbed into the boat, the wind died down" (Matt. 14:31–32).

- What does this story say about Jesus's leadership?

  _____ Jesus knew Peter would sink, so He was there to bail him out.

  _____ Jesus wanted to embarrass Peter by letting him sink.

  _____ Jesus wanted everyone to know that only He could walk on water.

  _____ Jesus had confidence in Peter and empowered him to do something spectacular.

- What leadership skills did Jesus use when Peter sank into the water?

  _____

  _____

Notice that Jesus acted immediately. He did not let Peter sink into the water and think about his mistake. It was Jesus's desire to let Peter know immediately that He was there to give the support he needed. Observe that Jesus *reached out His hand and caught him*. He used a personal touch to save the drowning apostle! Jesus knew that Peter's primary need was support, so He used His hand to save him. He reinforced His continued support when He said to him "You of little faith . . . why did you doubt?" In other words, Jesus is always there when we need Him.

It is also important to remember that after Jesus caught Peter, they were still outside the boat. The image we have of that scene is one where Jesus wraps His arms around Peter and walks him back into the boat.

Key Concepts

- It is easy to assume that journeymen—people who have acquired well-developed skills in performing a task or role—have progressed to a point where all they need from a leader is to be told when and where to apply their skills. The fact of the matter is that they may periodically become cautious, lose confidence, or have a diminished sense of enthusiasm for the job, due to a variety of reasons.

- Leaders who ignore the journeymen's needs for appreciation, encouragement, and inspiration do so at their peril.

A Point to Ponder

- Has there ever been a time when you felt underappreciated or unrecognized for a job well done because the attention was given to the "problem children?" What would have been the effects of a leader encouraging you with some heartfelt sign of appreciation?

_____

_____

_____

- What opportunities is God giving you to walk people back to the boat?

_____

_____

_____

Today's Second Topic
THE NEEDS OF A MASTER/TEACHER

Someone with fully-developed skills, confidence, and motivation to produce excellent results as an individual performer and the wisdom and insight to teach others needs the authorization opportunity to pass on what he or she knows to the next generation of learners.

Sending someone to act on your behalf is the highest validation of your trust in that person's competence and commitment. For example, when Jesus gave the Great Commission to His disciples, He assumed they were master/teachers and ready to perform on their own as fishers of men. He commissioned them to "go and make disciples of all nations, baptizing them in the name of the Father and of the Son and of the Holy Spirit, and teaching them to obey everything I have commanded you" (Matt. 28:19–20). While Jesus would not be physically present to direct and support the disciples as He had for three years, He did not turn His back on them. He promised, "I am with you always, to the very end of the age" (v. 20). Jesus promised not to leave the disciples alone to accomplish their task of being fishers of men. He promised He would always be available to them.

It is important not to confuse delegating with abdicating. Leaders who *abdicate* turn their backs and do not gather information on their own. They only become involved again if they hear bad news. But leaders who *delegate* stay in the information loop and are ready to help if they are called. Jesus delegated, but He did not abdicate. Jesus knew His disciples would need Him in the future, and He was ready when they called to support them when necessary.

An example of a master/teacher is the rehab department nurse calling on the stroke victim to demonstrate his skills with his cane and to encourage new patients who need to make the same journey from dependence to independence that he did.

Jesus and the Master/Teacher Disciples

It was Jesus's desire for His disciples to be able to be fully inspired and fully equipped for the task of being fishers of men. This is self-evident when we read about Peter spreading the Good News in Acts 2:36-41:

> "Therefore let all Israel be assured of this: God has made this Jesus, whom you crucified, both Lord and Christ." When the people heard this they were cut to the heart and said to Peter and the other apostles, "Brothers, what shall we do?" Peter replied "Repent and be baptized, every one of you, in the name of Jesus Christ for the forgiveness of your sins. And you will receive the gift of the Holy Spirit. The promise is for you and your children and for all who are far off—for all whom the Lord our God will call." With many other words he warned them; and he pleaded with them, "Save yourselves from this corrupt generation." Those who accepted his message were baptized, and about three thousand were added to their number that day.

Once again we can look at Peter and see how in Acts, under the anointing of the Holy Spirit, he showed that he was a master/teacher as he spoke to a crowd of thousands—and three thousand were baptized that day. He truly became a fisher of men. Peter had the knowledge to share the message of Jesus, and he also exhibited a high level of commitment as a master/teacher. Notice how Peter boldly shared the message of Jesus. He spoke with authority.

Look Inside

• Which statement best represents your desires for the people you lead?

_____ Keep them dependent on me so they will appreciate me

_____ Empower them to achieve their goals by becoming a master/teacher

In the question above, you don't have a lot of choices. Either you are empowering people to succeed or you are cautiously protecting your turf. You probably have been around both kinds of leaders.

• What does your leadership style produce?

_____ Frustrated individuals who do not have the competence or commitment to accomplish the assigned task

_____ People who are not only able to do the task on their own but who can also teach others

Can you imagine the benefits of having people around you who feel good about their jobs, are good at doing them, and are willing and able to teach others? That is what Jesus-like leadership produces.

Key Concepts

- Master/teachers need to be given the opportunity and challenge to pass on what they know to the next generation of learners—and they need your blessing.

- Sending someone to act on your behalf is the highest validation of your trust in that person's competence and commitment. It is also a sign that your vision of success in your own leadership includes serving future generations through those you have prepared.

- It is important not to confuse delegating with abdicating. Leaders who *abdicate* turn their backs on their people and do not gather information on their own. They only become involved again if they hear bad news. But leaders who *delegate* stay in the information loop and are ready to help if they are called.

- No one is totally a novice, apprentice, journeyman, or master/teacher in the things he or she does. At any one time in our work life or in one of our life role relationships, we could be at all four learning stages.

A Point to Ponder

Commissioning *to go and teach others in my name* is the highest form of recognition that a teacher can give a follower. Fulfilling the commission is the highest compliment and act of gratitude the student can afford the teacher. What are you doing to pass along that which has been given to you for the next generation? Are you ready to delegate both responsibility and authority to someone you know is ready for the challenge or are you holding back? If so, why?

_____

_____

_____

▶ Next Steps

What skills does a master/teacher need to be most effective?

_____

_____

_____

From your list above, identify the two skills you feel are your strongest skills. From the remaining skills, choose one that you most need to develop and identify your first step in that process.

_____

_____

_____

week five 5

THE *HANDS* OF A SERVANT LEADER, PART 2

Memory Verse for the Week

"Submit to one another out of reverence for Christ" (Eph. 5:21).

Whatever the problem, Jesus is the answer. Why? Because we have made a decision to submit our will to the will of God for our lives!

The issue is not just about commitment but about submission. Henry Blackaby, in his book *Spiritual Leadership*, says, "Some spiritual leaders try to be more committed. What they need is to be more submitted."[1] The first and most important decision you will ever make is to submit your life to God. Have you submitted your entire life to God? Have you asked Jesus to forgive you of your sins? If not, you can do it right now! This is the first decision you must make if you are going to lead like Jesus.

The next part of this decision is submitting your life to God and letting Him control every aspect of your life, including your leadership responsibilities. When Jesus said, "You will be blessed if you do them" (John 13:17), He meant it. This is a promise He gives to those who choose to follow His example of servant leadership. Submission to the will of God will mean the blessing of eternal life with Him, and our lives will be a blessing to the lives of the people we have the privilege of leading! We will leave a positive leadership legacy.

5 week five

day one | **1** •

THE EGO FACTOR

 Quote for Today

As a leader, the quickest remedy to the EGO factor in leader-follower relationships comes from seeking to acknowledge and combat your own vulnerabilities to pride and fear. The spiritual health of the leader is the wellspring from which a follower's trust and commitment flows.[2]

Ken Blanchard and Phil Hodges

 What God's Word Says

Therefore, as God's chosen people, holy and dearly loved, clothe yourselves with compassion, kindness, humility, gentleness and patience. Bear with each other and forgive whatever grievances you may have against one another. Forgive as the Lord forgave you. And over all these virtues put on love, which binds them all together in perfect unity. Let the peace of Christ rule in your hearts, since as members of one body you were called to peace. And be thankful. (Col. 3:12–15)

 Pause and Reflect

• If the passage above is the criteria for grading your spiritual effectiveness, what grade do you deserve and why?

_____

_____

_____

 A Prayer for Today

Lord, as I encounter others today, may Your grace, mercy, and peace be an extension of Your character through me. Teach me how to clothe myself in the grace-gifts of compassion, kindness, humility, gentleness, and patience so that at all times, for all reasons and in all seasons, people will see Jesus in me. In His Name, Amen!

Today's Topic
THE EGO FACTOR

A servant-hearted leader—whether in the office, at home, or in the community—confronted with an EGO-driven follower (learner) faces the daily challenge of ministering to the heart of the follower as well as of moving the learning process along. When your leadership is challenged or your motives and methods are mistrusted, keeping your own EGO in check can be a daunting chore. Reacting out of pride or fear can easily shortcut the learning process if you resort to exerting negative position-power to exert your will.

On the other hand, a servant-hearted follower confronted with an EGO-driven leader faces the daily challenge of being a positive witness to the leader while continuing to acquire the skills and experience needed to be productive and grow. It can be done, but it may be a hard, uphill climb. An EGO driven-leader can create disillusionment and cynicism in even the most servant-hearted follower, resulting in an ineffective learning process.

The true test of servant leadership begins when the EGO of the leader and the EGO of the follower engage one another. How well they recognize and overcome the pride and fear factors in their relationship will determine whether they move toward mutual satisfaction of commonly held goals or share in frustrations of their own making.

Take a look at the diagram below:

The EGO Factor in Leader-Follower Relationships

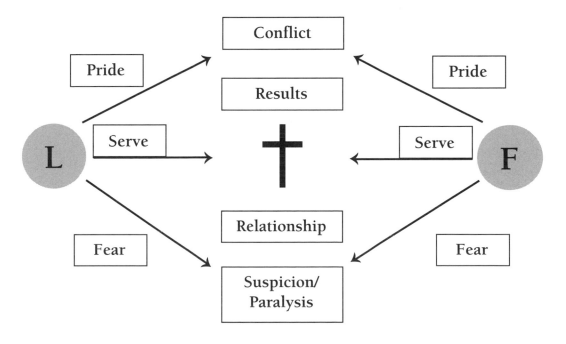

Four Ineffective Leader-Follower Relationships

The four **least** effective relationships between leader and follower are those in which the pride and fears of both leader and follower commingle to create conflict, suspicion, exploitation, and isolation.

1. Leader----->Fear----->Suspicion/Paralysis<-----Fear<-----Follower

When a leader and follower are both fearful in a relationship, they will be looking for warning signs that their fears are justified. Even initial evidence of goodwill and safety are looked on with suspicion. Negative assumptions about each other, based on stereotyping due to factors of age, race, position, ethic background, religion, and gender, can be a significant barrier to open communication.

Example: A leader who fears loss of position and a follower afraid of failure engage in relationship of mutual suspicion. An older white male manager is assigned to train an image-conscious minority employee on a fast-track development program.

Example: A parent who wants his child to know he is in charge and a child who does not want to admit he has done something wrong.

2. Leader ----->Pride----->Conflict/Competition<-----Pride<-----Follower

When a leader and a follower both bring their pride into a relationship, it is likely to become a test of wills. Instead of proceeding through cooperation and concessions, both parties seek to promote their position by winning arguments and tests of strength.

Example: A championship-winning coach with a ball-control strategy for winning meets a young superstar known for his brilliant individual skills.

Example: A parent who thinks she knows better what her teenage daughter could be doing and a teenager who is going through a *know-it-all* stage.

3. Leader----->Pride----->Exploitation<-----Fear<-----Follower

When a leader who is interested in imposing his will on the people under his control as an extension of his self-importance plays on the insecurities of the follower, the results are not likely to be for the common good.

Example: A results-driven pastor intimidates his congregation into voting for a new sanctuary.

Example: A parent who wants his son to listen to him because he is a parent and a teenager who is fearful of being seen by his peers as a mama's boy!

4. Leader----->Fear------>Manipulation<-----Pride<-----Follower

When an insecure leader succumbs to making unwise concessions or tries to exert position power to gain the cooperation of a strong-willed follower, the results are damaging.

Example: A micromanaging team leader who fears loss of control meets a prideful journeyman who responds with "malicious obedience" by complying with instructions that he knows are faulty.

Example: A parent who is afraid of the bad influences that may exist at school and a young son who is determined to demonstrate his independence.

Four Leader-Follower Relationships That Can Be Improved

There are four combinations of leader and follower EGOs that have specific challenges but can be **improved** if someone is willing to serve as an agent of change in the relationship. When that person is a leader it is a ministry opportunity and when the change agent is the follower it is a witnessing opportunity.

1. Leader----->Serve----->Ministry<-----Fear<-----Follower

A servant-hearted leader remains patient and reassuring by praising progress and honest effort when faced with followers who act out their insecurities.

Example: A physical therapist responds with patience and encouragement to outbursts of frustration and fear by a stroke victim learning to walk with a cane.

Example: A parent patiently waiting for a child to finish her temper tantrum.

2. Leader----->Serve----->Ministry<-----Pride<-----Follower

A servant-hearted leader models humility and strength of purpose and is willing to enforce standards and withstand challenges to his or her leadership.

Example: Jesus responds with humility (by washing their feet) to the pride of His disciples when they argue about who is to be greatest among them.

Example: A parent who does not get in a win/lose confrontation with a son over the family curfew.

3. Leader----->Pride ----->Witness<-----Serve<-----Follower

A follower is willing to risk a negative response from a leader in order to uphold a principle or correct an error.

Example: The prophet Nathan confronts King David regarding his misconduct with Bathsheba.

Example: A child confronts his father about his drinking and driving.

4. Leader----->Fear----->Witness<-----Serve<-----Follower

A follower responds to the insecurities of a leader with humility and respect, without foregoing principle.

Example: As an expression of his allegiance and respect, David, while being pursued by a fear-driven King Saul, forgoes the opportunity to kill him when he had the chance.

Example: A child patiently makes allowances for her a parent, who is fearful about her going away to school.

The Ideal Leader-Follower Relationship

Servant-hearted Leader----->Results and Relationship<-----Servant-hearted Follower

The **ideal**, most productive relationship between leader and follower occurs when a servant-hearted leader and a servant-hearted follower engage one another in an atmosphere of mutual service and trust. It is when a clear sense of purpose, process, and practice passes from the leader and is received and owned by the follower. The follower, in turn, responds with trust and willingness to perform and take instruction.

Example: Jesus glorified God by completing the work that had been set before Him to do (John 17:4).

Example: A husband and wife living out their marriage vows in a relationship of mutual respect and service.

Overcoming the EGO Factor in Leader-Follower Relationships

As a leader, the quickest remedy to the EGO factor in leader-follower relationships comes from seeking to acknowledge and combat your own vulnerabilities to pride and fear. The spiritual health of the leader is the wellspring from which a follower's trust and commitment flows. If you seek to inspire and equip others to higher standards of performance and commitment, the best first step is modeling integrity in your own journey in the same direction.

As a follower whose self-worth and security is grounded in God's unconditional love and promises, keeping a big-picture perspective of what is to be gained or lost in responding to poor treatment by an EGO-driven leader can truly "turn lemons into lemonade."

- Quickly match the numbered expected outcomes with the right Leader/Follower relationship. (Note: #6 Ministry and # 2 Positive Witness will both be the right match for two of the Leader/Follower Relationships.)

Expected Outcome Leader/Follower Relationship

1. Manipulation	____ Pride/Pride
2. Positive Witness	____ Pride/Serve
3. Positive results and relationship	____ Pride/Fear
4. Conflict	____ Fear/Fear
5. Paralysis/Isolation	____ Fear/Serve
6. Ministry	____ Serve/Serve
7. Exploitation	____ Fear/Pride
	____ Serve/Fear
	____ Serve/Pride

(Answers 4, 2, 7, 5, 3, 1, 6, 6)

Key Concepts

- The quickest remedy to the EGO factor in leader-follower relationships comes from seeking to acknowledge and combat your own vulnerabilities to pride and fear.

- We all fall short of perfection, and every day we have to confront our own EGO issues that can get us off purpose and impact the leader and follower/learner relationship.

- If both the leader and the follower are willing to share their own vulnerabilities and support one another in keeping on track, then the best of all results is possible—the true win-win-win situation: the leader wins, the follower wins, and God wins!

A Point to Ponder

Think about a life role situation that you experienced when the results were hurt feelings and poor results. How would you diagnose the motivations of the Leader and the Follower in this incident using the combinations of Pride, Fear and Serve?

- A time when I experienced a negative Leader /Follower relationship was when I

_____

_____

_____

- The motivation that drove the leader's behavior in this incident was _____.
- The motivation that drove the follower's behavior in this incident was _____.
- The combined effect of the Leader's and the Follower's attitude toward one another was _____.
- The impact on productivity of this relationship was _____.
- How could I have changed the outcome of this incident by altaring my own pride or fears?

_____

_____

_____

Next Steps

Think about the most important personal relationship you have. As you look at the EGO Factor diagram on page 119, consider how you might move this relationship into a win-win-win situation where God wins, you win, and the other person wins. If it is already an ideal relationship, then spend this time celebrating!

THE EGO FACTOR IN THE FOUR LEARNING STAGES

❝ Quote for Today

Aware of the potential EGO barriers in their relationship and willing to confront them, the leader and the follower can seek individually and together to overcome these barriers through personal preparation, open communication, and a mutual commitment to serve one another and their relationship. One unique resource at the disposal of the followers of Jesus is the active participation of the Holy Spirit as Counselor and Guide.[3]

Ken Blanchard and Phil Hodges

What God's Word Says

But the Counselor, the Holy Spirit, whom the Father will send in my name, will teach you all things and will remind you of everything I have said to you. (John 14:26)

Pause and Reflect

It's easy to trust our education, training, instincts, business savvy, etc., when faced with leadership issues. What might be the end result of an intentional focus on the Holy Spirit?

_____

_____

_____

A Prayer for Today

Father God, I want to glorify You by doing the work that You have set before me today in a way that honors You and Your love for me and all the people You put in my path. Help me be quickly aware of the temptations to act in a prideful and fearful way in response to others. Guide me in Your love and truth to be a servant-hearted leader or follower. In Jesus's name, Amen!

Today's Topic
THE EGO FACTOR IN THE FOUR LEARNING STAGES

As we have emphasized, we all fall short of perfection, and every day we have to confront our own EGO issues that can get us off purpose and can impact the leader and follower/learner relationship. So let's see if we can anticipate the EGO issues that leaders and followers face at each of the four learning stages:

EGO Issues at the Novice Stage

Learner/Novice EGO Issues

Fear of failure

Fear of inadequacy

Fear of looking foolish

False pride in position

False pride due to prior performance

Lack of trust in the leader or the method of training

Teacher/Leader EGO Issues

Impatience in teaching fundamentals

Frustration with slow progress

Temptation for premature delegation

Making quick judgments of potential

Fear of failure

EGO Issues at the Apprentice Stage

Learner/Apprentice EGO Issues

Discouragement with lack of progress

Impatience with the learning process

Loss of faith in the learning process

Fear of failure

Fear of inadequacy

Loss of faith in the leader

Diminished enthusiasm for the task

Teacher/Leader EGO Issues

Fear of failure

Frustration with lack of enthusiasm

Unrealistic expectations of people

Fear of the opinion of others

Fear of criticism

Fear of loss of position

EGO Issues at the Journeyman Stage

Learner/Journeyman EGO Issues

Fear of failure when moving into new situations

Fear of success in expanded use of skills

Burnout—loss of enthusiasm

Fear of obsolescence

Fear of competition

Fear of exploitation

Teacher/Leader EGO Issues

Lack of sensitivity to lost enthusiasm

Overuse of competence

Fear of intimacy required to deal with the individual issues

Fear of the learner surpassing the teacher

Fear of confronting slips in performance

EGO Issues at the Master/Teacher Stage

Learner/Master EGO Issues

Complacency with current personal knowledge and skills

Unwillingness to take criticism or direction

Arrogance

Misuse of skills for self-serving purposes

Teacher/Leader EGO Issues

Fear of personal obsolescence when the learner can do what you do

Unwillingness to share information or recognition

Fear of loss of control

Look Inside

Review the Leader and Follower EGO issues shown above and create your own top three EGO challenges as a leader and as a follower at each learning stage.

My Top Three EGO Issues at the Novice Stage

Learner/Novice EGO Issues   *Teacher/Leader EGO Issues*

1 _____   _____

2 _____   _____

3 _____   _____

My Top Three EGO Issues at the Apprentice Stage

Learner/Apprentice EGO Issues   *Teacher/Leader EGO Issues*

1 _____   _____

2 _____   _____

3 _____   _____

My Top Three EGO Issues at the Journeyman Stage

Learner/Journeyman EGO Issues   *Teacher/Leader EGO Issues*

1 _____   _____

2 _____   _____

3 _____   _____

My Top Three EGO Issues at the Master/Teacher Stage

Learner/Master EGO Issues   *Teacher/Leader EGO Issues*

1 _____   _____

2 _____   _____

3 _____   _____

- What EGO challenges repeat themselves at each stage when you are acting as a Leader or as a Follower? What steps will you to take to altar these?

_____

_____

Key Concepts

- Once aware of the potential EGO barriers in their relationship, a leader and follower can seek to overcome these barriers through personal preparation, open communication, and a mutual commitment to serve one another in their relationship.
- Both a leader and a follower have the opportunity to honor their own higher purpose by seeking to serve rather than be served.

A Point to Ponder

One unique resource at the disposal of the followers of Jesus is the active participation of the Holy Spirit as Counselor and Guide. Jesus promised in John 14:26, "the Counselor, the Holy Spirit, whom the Father will send in My name, will teach you all things and will remind you of everything I have said to you."

In the Appendix, beginning on page 165, there are a series of prayers for both leaders and followers as they progress from novice to master/teacher. We want to encourage you to use these preemptive prayers whenever you are about to enter a leader/learner situation. It will make a powerful difference.

Staying on Purpose

As we have emphasized, even if you, as a leader or follower/learner, are committed to serve rather than be served, every day your EGO is waiting to get you off course and focus your energy on being self-serving. In week 6, we will take a look at some of the habits that were essential to Jesus's renewing and affirming His daily walk of submission and obedience as a servant and leader.

Next Steps

When a leader and a follower are fearful of one another, what is most likely to happen? Give an example that you have observed or experienced.

_____

_____

_____

_____

What steps could you take to remove fear from a situation as a follower?

_____

_____

_____

As a leader?

_____

_____

_____

THE WAY OF FORGIVENESS

 Quote for Today

Leaders seeking to grow and develop people as an end goal of equal importance to results, need a healthy capacity to forgive, correct, and move on.[4]

Ken Blanchard and Phil Hodges

 What God's Word Says

For if you forgive men when they sin against you, your heavenly Father will also forgive you. But if you do not forgive men their sins, your Father will not forgive your sins. (Matt. 6:14–15)

Pause and Reflect

• What makes it so difficult for leaders to forgive others? To what extent is this an issue in your life?

_____

_____

_____

_____

_____

_____

 A Prayer for Today

Lord, forgiveness is key to every area of my life. I know that You have forgiven me and I'm grateful. I ask now for the capacity to forgive any and all who need forgiveness from me. May I be gracious to them as You have been gracious to me and in so doing both they and I will find freedom. In Jesus's Name, Amen!

Today's Topic
THE WAY OF FORGIVENESS

Why is forgiveness an important aspect of leading like Jesus? Jesus established the centrality of forgiveness in His leadership when He cried out from the cross, "Father, forgive them, for they do not know what they are doing . . ." (Luke 23:34). One of the most frequent tests of whether we have the heart attitude required to lead like Jesus is how we deal with the failures of those we lead to perform according to plan. Remember, getting things roughly right is simply part of the learning process that precedes getting things exactly right on a consistent basis. Pride and fear will, from time to time, raise their ugly heads and cause people to go off course during the process of learning or implementing an assigned task.

Leaders, seeking to grow and develop people as an end goal of equal importance to results, need a healthy capacity to forgive, correct, and move on. EGO-driven leaders, impatient for results, are quick to judge and discount less-than-perfect efforts as failure rather than to forgive and redirect.

Forgiveness is a supernatural act, not a natural response to being hurt or let down. It is an act of the will of one who has surrendered control to a higher court of judgment. Forgiveness is a hallmark of what it means to lead like Jesus. He taught forgiveness to His disciples, He practiced it with those who betrayed Him, and He granted it willingly to those who participated in His death on the cross. As leaders, the journey of forgiveness must start with us. Unlike Jesus, we all fall short of 100 percent perfection in our journey as leaders. Sometimes we make mistakes that could have been avoided. Sometimes we say or do things in the heat of the moment that we regret. If our EGO is wrapped up in our performance and the opinion of others, we will be unable to forgive our own shortcomings, let alone anyone else's.

The opposite of forgiveness is judgment. Your motivation for doing something is as important as what you do. Jesus gave definite instruction on the subject of condemning judgment.

In Luke 6:37-42 we read:

> Do not judge, and you will not be judged. Do not condemn, and you will not be condemned. Forgive, and you will be forgiven. Give, and it will be given to you. A good measure, pressed down, shaken together and running over, will be poured into your lap. For with the measure you use, it will be measured to you . . . Why do you look at the speck of sawdust in your brother's eye and pay no attention to the plank in your own eye? How can you say to your brother, "Brother, let me take the speck out of your eye," when you yourself fail to see the plank in your own eye? You hypocrite, first take the plank out of your eye, and then you will see clearly to remove the speck from your brother's eye.

Judgment is pointing out a fault with a view to condemnation. On the other hand, discernment is pointing out a fault with a view to correction or restoration. When we withhold forgiveness is it because we are sincerely trying to correct or restore—or is it because there is some benefit to us in condemning?

Look Inside

- How would people who have wronged you describe your usual response?

  Quick to Forgive / Slow to Judge _____ or Quick to Judge/ Slow to Forgive _____

- Why is it so easy to accept God's forgiveness and so hard to forgive others?

  _____

  _____

  _____

Key Concepts

- Forgiveness is agreeing to live with the consequences of another person's sin. You will live with those consequences whether you like it or not; your only choice is whether you will do so in the bitterness of unforgiveness or the freedom of forgiveness.

- You don't forgive someone for their sake: you do it for your sake, so you can be free.

- Forgiveness is a particular dimension of an even broader element of the leadership of Jesus—grace.

A Point to Ponder

The price of forgiveness is letting go of the right to require either payment or an apology for a wrongdoing. Whom do you need to forgive in order to restore a relationship with someone who let you down?

Next Steps

Why is forgiveness an important aspect of leadership?

  _____

  _____

  _____

What is the price that must be paid if true forgiveness is to have an impact on the future of a relationship?

  _____

  _____

Who do you need to forgive in order to restore a productive relationship? What step do you need to take to begin the reconciliation?

_____

_____

_____

THE WAY OF GRACE

 Quote for Today

Grace is the currency of all true relationships.

- Father Joseph Fox

 **What God's Word Says**

From the fullness of his grace we have all received one blessing after another. For the law was given through Moses; grace and truth came through Jesus Christ. (John 1:16-17)

❚❚ Pause and Reflect

The entire Bible reveals God's concept of leadership. The Law has its purpose, and grace has its purpose. Think about your role as a leader. Describe a time when you extended grace to someone who made a mistake.

_____

_____

_____

_____

_____

_____

_____

 A Prayer for Today

Lord, grace, fully extended by You, deserves to be fully extended by me to others. Help me to see others as an opportunity to dispense grace, accepting them as they are and urging them and myself to become all that we can become in You. In Jesus's Name, Amen!

Today's Topic
THE WAY OF GRACE

The key to ministering to followers who are struggling with pride or fear, and being a positive witness to leaders inflicted by the same vices, is the power of grace.

Grace extends unrestrained goodwill to others in celebration of their inherent dignity that comes from being made in God's image and as the objects of His affection. Grace is at work in relationships when we are fully present to one another, accept our mutual limitations, and exchange mutual efforts to enhance one another's well-being. It is only in intimacy that grace abounds.

God has reached out in the most profound way to restore our intimate relationship with Him. Even when we walk away from Him in our sin, His grace abounds in that "while we were still sinners, Christ died for us" (Rom. 5:8). During His season of leadership, Jesus constantly reached out in unrestrained fellowship and acceptance to heal and restore people to relationships of grace and acceptance. To lead like Jesus, we must come to understand the spiritual dynamics of our relationships as both leaders and followers, so that we may be agents of grace in a like manner.

Grace can be thought of as composed of three interdependent elements: presence, acceptance, and community.

To extend grace to someone is to first be *fully present* in the moment with them. Grace and multi-tasking rarely exist in the same moment. You will easily remember those people in your life who, when they spoke to you even in a crowd, made you feel as if you were the only person on the planet. Extending the grace of presence with no other motives than to seek to understand and to encourage open communication has great healing power in relationships that are adrift.

A second component of grace is *acceptance* of the mutual limitations of the moment and the people involved. A leader may be new at leading and a follower may be hard of hearing. A follower may need details to be willing to try and the leader may be excited about the big picture but short on information about what to do next. Willingness to acknowledge and accept limitations as a mutual responsibility is both humbling and also the doorway to discovering new strengths and opportunities to grow.

A third aspect of grace is *seeking to serve* the highest common purpose in both the results and relationship—to serve rather than be served, to do the work that God has set out for you to do together, to love one another as you have been loved, to be salt and light, to awaken a sense of God in the lives of others, and to glorify God.

Look Inside

- Describe what might happen if, for the next thirty days, you were fully focused on enriching your relationships with your loved ones?

_____

_____

_____

• What would happen if you bridged the gap between yourself and those you are called to serve who are less knowledgeable, less committed, but more successful than you are in your work?

_____

_____

_____

• How would the results and relationships in your team or family be different if the people you serve felt your commitment to their best interest was your number one priority?

_____

_____

_____

Key Concepts

• The key to ministering to followers who are struggling with pride or fear, and being a positive witness to leaders inflicted by the same vices, is the power of grace in all relationships.

• To extend grace to someone is to first be *fully present* in the moment with them.

• A second component of grace is *acceptance* of the mutual limitations of the moment and the people involved.

• A third aspect of grace is *seeking to serve* the highest common purpose in both results and relationship.

A Point to Ponder

Think of the impact of grace in your most important relationship. Think about keeping that relationship in the moment. Think about accepting the reality of your inability to add or detract from the love that is extended to you or to do anything of eternal value outside that relationship. Think about the joy and freedom of knowing that you can trust without doubt, and surrender without fear, to the goodness of the One who has always had your best interest as His highest priority. How would you say thank you for amazing grace?

_____

_____

▶ Next Steps

Describe in your own words what it means as a leader to extend grace to someone under your influence.

_____

_____

_____

Does someone under your influence need grace extended to them now? What will you do about it?

_____

_____

_____

5

THE POWER OF APOLOGY

Quote for Today

There are two phrases that people should use more often. They could change the world: Thank you, and I am sorry.

Dorothy Blanchard (Ken's Mother)

What God's Word Says

When he came to his senses, he said, "How many of my father's hired men have food to spare, and here I am starving to death! I will set out and go back to my father and say to him: Father, I have sinned against heaven and against you. I am no longer worthy to be called your son; make me like one of your hired men." So he got up and went to his father. (Luke 15:17–20)

Pause and Reflect

- Describe a time when you have had to ask for forgiveness. What was the most difficult part of that experience?

_____

_____

_____

_____

_____

A Prayer for Today

Father God, I realize that I will always be a work in progress and prone to make mistakes because of pride and fear. Help me honor You and Your unconditional love by seeking to heal any wounds I have created through accepting responsibility and apologizing; and accepting whatever response I get with love and humility. In Jesus's Name, Amen!

Today's Topic

THE POWER OF APOLOGY

Jesus said, "Be perfect, therefore, as your heavenly Father is perfect" (Matt. 5:48). This is a high standard that Jesus set for us, and we need to remember that we all fall short of it. As you seek to employ what you have been learning about leading like Jesus, making mistakes will be inevitable. The way in which you respond to the knowledge of your own mistakes will be as clear an indicator of the condition of your heart as how you handle criticism and praise.

The Parable of the Prodigal Son provides a rich source of wisdom on the core elements of an authentic apology. The first aspect of a meaningful apology is a true sense that you have done something wrong, which has negatively impacted someone else. Notice the young man in the parable identified both his earthly Father and his Heavenly Father as being wronged by his bad behavior. When prideful leaders come face-to-face with their own imperfections two common first reactions are denial and rationalization. They may try to look the other way because what they see is too painful to their own self-image or push the blame onto someone or something else. In each of these reactions there is at least a struggle to deal with the truth. A more destructive response to a mistake is when we try to make it go away by lying to ourselves that it really wasn't that big a deal or maybe not even a mistake at all.

As you journey on the path of leading like Jesus, a natural experience will be to become more aware of the harm that you do as well as the progress you are making. The burden would become unbearable if it were not for the fact that surrendered confession to an all-forgiving and loving God is always an alternative to denial and rationalization.

Seeking God's forgiveness through prayer and confession will make it much easier to deal with the people you have wronged, who may not be as forgiving.

Servant leaders must be willing to model accountability if they are to inspire it in others. When they make mistakes, they must be willing to pay the consequences in order to retain their integrity and build trust. The young man in the parable, after coming to his senses, was willing to surrender his status as a family member and assume the role of a servant as just payment for his mistakes.

Look Inside

- When faced with the fact that you need to apologize, what has been your most frequent response?

    _____ Keep quiet and hope they don't notice

    _____ Spend more time working up an excuse than finding the right time and place to apologize

    _____ Try to avoid apologizing until you have done something praise worthy to balance the bad news

    _____ Make issuing a sincere apology a high priority item and do it as quickly as possible

Key Concepts

- An apology always starts with recognition and acceptance that you did something wrong.
- Seeking God's forgiveness first through prayer and confession will make it much easier to deal with the people you have wronged, who may not be as forgiving.

A Point to Ponder

- What conditions for your forgiveness do you require be met before you will forgive? What conditions did God place on His forgiveness of you?

_____

_____

_____

- Do you believe Jesus when He says, "For if you forgive men when they sin against you, your heavenly Father will also forgive you. But if you do not forgive men their sins, your Father will not forgive your sins" (Matt. 6:14–15)? And if so, are there some issues and relationships you need to attend to right away?

_____

_____

_____

Next Steps

Give an example of a time when someone apologized to you. How did it make you feel? What did it do to the relationship?

_____

_____

_____

Is there someone to whom you need to apologize? Make a list below of the points you want to make as you speak with him/her. Next, schedule a meeting with that person to follow through.

_____

_____

_____

week six

THE *HABITS* OF A SERVANT LEADER

6

Memory Verse for the Week

"But his delight is in the law of the Lord, and on his law he meditates day and night. He is like a tree planted by streams of water, which yields its fruit in season and whose leaf does not wither. Whatever he does prospers"

(Ps. 1:2-3).

As Jesus moved through His season of earthly leadership, He was under constant pressure and temptation to be drawn off course by the failings of His friends, His family and His enemies. Through it all Jesus modeled five key habits to stay on track with His mission. These habits were the primary antidote He applied to counter the opposing forces in His life:

- Solitude
- Prayer
- Knowledge and Application of Scripture
- Accepting and Responding to God's Unconditional Love
- Maintaining Accountability Relationships

Adopting these same habits is essential for those who seek to follow Jesus as their role model for leadership. Jesus didn't try to lead without them, and neither should we if we want to lead like Him.

For Jesus, these habits flowed effortlessly from His very nature. They were the distinctive core elements of His manner and way. For us they do not come naturally. They must begin as disciplines we must practice before they can become habits.

6 week six

day one | **6** •

THE HABIT OF SOLITUDE

Quote of the Day

Only alone can I draw close enough to God to discover His secrets.

- George Washington Carver

What God's Word Says

That evening after sunset the people brought to Jesus all the sick and demon-possessed. The whole town gathered at the door, and Jesus healed many who had various diseases. He also drove out many demons, but he would not let the demons speak because they knew who he was. Very early in the morning, while it was still dark, Jesus got up, left the house and went off to a solitary place, where he prayed. Simon and his companions went to look for him, and when they found him, they exclaimed: "Everyone is looking for you!" Jesus replied, "Let us go somewhere else—to the nearby villages—so I can preach there also. That is why I have come. (Mark 1:32–38)

Solitude is a countercultural and challenging behavior. It draws us into the very place from which so much of our efforts are designed to help us escape – being truly alone with God without an agenda. It is a rare and often unsettling feeling to stop doing and just be.

Pause and Reflect

• Describe a time when you were alone with God. Why is it difficult to make being alone with Him a priority?

_____

_____

A Prayer for Today

As you pray, sit quietly, listening to what God might be saying to you. As you progress through the week, gradually increase the time you spend alone listening to God.

Today's Topic
THE HABIT OF SOLITUDE

We live in a noisy hurry, running from place to place, somehow feeling as if multitasking is a status symbol. We seldom pay attention to one thing at a time—including God! Somehow, we have lost the ability to be quiet and still.

Jesus found value in solitude—being completely alone with God, away from all human contact. Solitude is stepping outside your noisy world to breathe in some fresh air. Solitude is refreshing. It is resting in God's presence. Solitude is being alone without being lonely. Sometimes doing nothing is the best thing you can do for your people and for yourself. Jesus modeled solitude as an integral strategic component of his manner of leadership. Consider the following:

- When preparing for the tests of leadership and public ministry, Jesus spent forty days alone in the desert. (Matt. 4:1–11)
- Before choosing His twelve apostles from among His followers, Jesus spent the entire night alone in the desert hills. (Luke 6:12–13)
- When He received the news of the death of John the Baptist, Jesus withdrew in a boat to a lonely place. (Matt. 14:13)
- After the miraculous feeding of the five thousand, Jesus went up in the hills by Himself. (Matt. 14:23)

It was in these times of preparing to lead, making important decisions, handling bad news, and dealing with praise and recognition, that Jesus modeled for us the value of spending time alone to seek recalibration of our spiritual instruments, for finding the true north of God's will and pleasure.

The most powerful example of the critical role that solitude played in the life and leadership of Jesus is described in today's scripture passage from Mark 1:35: "Very early in the morning, while it was still dark, Jesus got up, left the house and went to a solitary place, where he prayed." These words stand between Jesus and the temptation to spend His precious time doing the good and popular thing instead of doing the primary work for which He had come. Imagine the intense compassion Jesus had for the sick and demon-possessed people whom He would have to leave unhealed. Imagine how strong the temptation would have been for Jesus to stay and use His healing powers to the delight of all. It would have, by any human standard, been a good use of His time and capabilities. But from God's perspective it was not the best thing He could do. What allowed Jesus to resist doing this good work and pick the best? We believe that in solitude and prayer, away from the hopes and hurts of those who looked to Him with high and compelling expectations, that Jesus again received the answers of the best use of the next day from the Father.

Look Inside

When was the last time you spent a significant amount of time in solitude on purpose, without a to-do, think, or pray list, and sat quietly in God's presence and listened to His still, small voice? If you can't remember, you now have a clue why your life and leadership may seem so hindered and unsatisfying. If you can remember and it was more than a week ago, you need to update your plans for the immediate future.

In our Lead Like Jesus Encounters (see page 173) we ask participants to take forty-five minutes of solitude—a time when they do not talk to anyone, use their computer or PDA, cell phone, or any other devices. We ask them to begin by putting their hands palms down on their knees and think of anything they are excited or concerned about. As an item appears in their mind, they are requested to ceremonially put it down at the foot of The Cross. When they have put down everything they can think of, we ask them to then turn their hands upward in a posture of receiving. As they remain still, it is suggested that they focus on an aspect of the character of God such, as His mercy, love, holiness, power, or creativity. We instruct them to listen without any agenda. Almost everyone who participates in this activity finds it both difficult and powerful. The reality is that most of us spend little if any time in solitude. And yet if we don't, how can God have a chance to talk with us?

- What changes in your life routine would you need to make in order to allow time for solitude?

  _____

  _____

  _____

- What activities stand between you and your time alone with God?

  _____

  _____

  _____

 ## Next Steps

Devote a minimum of thirty-five minutes during the next week to be still and in solitude listening to God. Be prepared to share your experience with the members of your small group.

THE HABIT OF PRAYER

 Quote for Today

Don't bother to give God instructions; just report for duty.[1]

- Corrie ten Boom

 What God's Word Says

Do not be anxious about anything, but in everything, by prayer and petition, with thanksgiving, present your requests to God. And the peace of God, which transcends all understanding, will guard your hearts and your minds in Christ Jesus. (Phil. 4:6–7)

 Pause and Reflect

- The antidote to worry is prayer. What is one thing you are worried about and why is it not a matter of prayer?

_____

_____

_____

_____

 A Prayer for Today

Lord, I need to keep faithfully in tune with You all day, every day. Sometimes the cares and woes of life keep me away. Sometimes, I feel that I can do it on my own. In both of these ways and in others as well, I'm so wrong. I need You every moment of my day and my life. Draw me closer to You than ever before. Make my every moment a conscious awareness of my need to communicate with You in prayer. Help me to carve out time in every day just to sit quietly with You so that I might know You and Your plans for my life, and so that I might be prepared for what life will throw at me. In Jesus's Name, Amen!

Today's Topic
THE HABIT OF PRAYER

If solitude is the most elusive of habits for us to develop, prayer is the one that requires the most unlearning and revision of old habits and patterns. Prayer is an essential act of the will that demonstrates whether we are really serious about living and leading like Jesus. Without it, we will never be able to open the way for connecting our plans and efforts with God's plan for His kingdom or engaging the spiritual resources that Jesus promised in the work of the Holy Spirit. Seeking God's will through prayer, waiting in faith for an answer, acting in accordance with that answer, and being at peace with the outcome all call for a level of spiritual maturity that will keep anyone seeking to lead like Jesus in the posture of a lifelong learner. The one thing that is most instructive in showing us how and where leaders might take their followers is found in their prayer life, as the nature and objects of our prayers determine whether we are being EGO-driven or are glorifying God.

To become a Lead-Like-Jesus leader you will face some leadership challenges. Let us examine the example Jesus gave us to follow. Nowhere in the Bible are the elements of what it means to pray like Jesus more powerfully provided for us than in the dark hours of the night before He was betrayed. This was a time when the temptation to abandon His mission was at an almost unbearable level.

> Then Jesus went with his disciples to a place called Gethsemane, and he said to them, "Sit here while I go over there and pray." He took Peter and the two sons of Zebedee along with him, and he began to be sorrowful and troubled. Then he said to them, "My soul is overwhelmed with sorrow to the point of death. Stay here and keep watch with me." Going a little farther, he fell with his face to the ground and prayed, "My Father, if it is possible, may this cup be taken from me. Yet not as I will, but as you will" (Matt. 26:36–39).

Where Did Jesus Pray and Why?

He went off by himself for prayer. A troubled soul finds the most ease when it is alone with God, who understands the broken language of sighs and groans. While alone with God, Jesus could freely pour His heart out to the Father without restraint. Christ has taught and modeled for us that secret prayer is to be done secretly.

What Was His Posture in Prayer?

He fell on His face before His Father, indicating the agony He was in, the extremity of His sorrow, and His humility in prayer. At other times Jesus prayed looking up to heaven, with His eyes open, or kneeling. The posture of the heart is more important than the posture of the body, but prostrating our physical selves before God helps our heart posture.

What Did He Ask in Prayer?

Jesus asked, "If it is possible, let this cup be taken from Me." He was asking if He could avoid the suffering ahead. But notice the way Jesus couched His request: "if it is possible." He knew the Father and left the answer to Him when He said, "Yet not as I will, but as You will." Although Jesus keenly sensed the bitter sufferings He was to undergo, He freely subjugated His desire to the Father. He based His own willingness upon the Father's will.

What Was the Answer to His Prayer?

His answer was that the will of the Father would be done. The cup did not pass from Him, for He withdrew the petition in deference to His Father's will. But He got an answer to His prayer. He was strengthened for the mission He had come to fulfill: "An angel from heaven appeared to him and strengthened him" (Luke 22:43).

As leaders, doing the right thing for the right reasons might require us to drink the bitter cup in form of ridicule, rejection, and anger. Our human tendency will be to try to avoid the pain. Leading like Jesus calls us to proceed in faith and to trust in God's grace to provide us with the courage to do the right thing and finish the task.

The Power of Preemptive Prayer

In leading like Jesus, prayer should never be restricted or relegated to our last resort in times of deep distress. It is our most powerful, most immediately accessible, most useful preemptive resource for responding to the moment-to-moment challenges of both good and bad times.

As you look forward to the work of the day, you will probably find that you are, in some situations, acting as a leader and in others as a follower. You will also find that you may be dealing with varying levels of development, both yours and those of the people with whom you are working. For instance, you may be called on to play the role of a coach to a group of seasoned people who have lost their enthusiasm for an important but routine task, and at the same time you are in the role of a novice learning a new computer system from someone three levels down from you in your organization. Both roles will have EGO challenges, and both are opportunities to serve. Each can be subject to the energizing power of preemptive prayer. It might be a good idea to transform today's to-do list into today's prayer list and let God into the picture.

Look Inside

Take a few moments to apply some brutal honesty in answering the questions below, after reading the instructions Jesus gave to His followers about prayer:

> And when you pray, do not be like the hypocrites, for they love to pray standing in the synagogues and on the street corners to be seen by men. I tell you the truth, they have received their reward in full. But when you pray, go into your

room, close the door and pray to your Father, who is unseen. Then your Father, who sees what is done in secret, will reward you. And when you pray, do not keep on babbling like pagans, for they think they will be heard because of their many words. Do not be like them, for your Father knows what you need before you ask him. This, then, is how you should pray: "Our Father in heaven, hallowed be your name, your kingdom come, your will be done on earth as it is in heaven. Give us today our daily bread. Forgive us our debts, as we also have forgiven our debtors.

And lead us not into temptation, but deliver us from the evil one." For if you forgive men when they sin against you, your heavenly Father will also forgive you. But if you do not forgive men their sins, your Father will not forgive your sins. (Matt. 6:5–15)

- How often is prayer your first response to a temptation or a challenge rather than your last resort?

  _____

  _____

- What is it that leads you to prayer?

  _____

  _____

- Where do you go to pray?

  _____

  _____

- For what do you most often pray?

  _____

  _____

- How do you know God's answer to your prayer?

  _____

  _____

Key Concepts

- The one thing that is most instructive about how and where leaders might take their followers is found in their prayer life.
- Prayer is an essential act of the will that demonstrates whether we are really serious about living and leading like Jesus.

- Prayer should be our natural first response rather than our last resort.
- In prayer, God has given us the most powerful, most immediately available resource for responding to the moment-to-moment challenges of both good and bad times.
- Prayer honors God.

 ## A Point to Ponder

- What is the major difference between the following two attitudes toward prayer: "Well, all we can do now is pray," and "The first thing we should do is pray?"

_____

_____

- Which one is closest to your view of prayer up to now?

_____

_____

 ## Next Steps

Begin keeping a prayer journal so that you can be reminded of the daily prayers God constantly is answering.

week six

day three | 3 • • •

THE HABIT OF KNOWING AND APPLYING SCRIPTURE

❝ Quote for Today

Most people are bothered by those passages in Scripture that they cannot understand; but as for me, I always noticed that the passages in Scripture that trouble me most are those that I do understand.[2]

Mark Twain

📖 What God's Word Says

> All Scripture is God-breathed and is useful for teaching, rebuking, correcting and training in righteousness, so that the man of God may be thoroughly equipped for every good work. (2 Tim. 3:16–17)

Take a look at the passage above and fill in the blanks:

1. God's Word originated with _____.

2. God's Word is useful for _____.

3. The personal benefit of God's Word is _____.

⏸ Pause and Reflect

• What are some biblical instructions our culture doesn't support? Do you find yourself defending your actions with rationalization or challenging your actions through Scripture?

_____

_____

_____

🙌 A Prayer for Today:

Father God, I acknowledge the love letter of your truth that you have sent to me in the form of your Holy Word. Help me to read it with an open heart and store its wisdom in my memory that I may live out its message in the way that I influence others. In Jesus' Name. Amen!

Today's Topic
KNOWING AND APPLYING SCRIPTURE

Skeptics argue that God's Word was written by men and, therefore, is fallible. It is true that God's Word was *recorded* by men, but it originated with God. Because it is God's personal letter to those He loves, it has tremendous benefit for His people—it teaches, corrects, and trains us in His ways. When we are taught, corrected, and trained, our thoughts and actions will be more like those of God. Therefore, we will be able to do something that, by nature, we can't do—good works.

So, what is *good*? By the time Micah 6:8 was written, good already had been established. Micah said that God already had told the people what was good. There wasn't more to come. Good didn't need to be socially redefined, legislated, or discussed. The short version of good is simply this—love God and love other people.

Think about it—four of the Ten Commandments deal with our relationship with God and six of them address how we interact with each other. When asked what the greatest commandment was, Jesus replied not with one of the Ten Commandments but with the *shema*—a saying rooted in Deuteronomy that reminded the Jews to love God with their entire beings. Jesus then added practical application of that instruction—love others. We see it over and over throughout Scripture—love God, love others. Of course, like the Jews, we have complicated the simple and turned it into a complex collection of rules and regulations that are debated and discussed by subsets of the family of God. Every denomination has its interpretation (and often complication) of the simple truths of God's Word. The fact is that God's Word is built upon this simple foundation: love God and love other people.

If you only use the Bible to study and apply the practical wisdom it contains about dealing with people and overcoming your internal challenges, it still would stand absolutely alone as the greatest book ever written. But it is so much more than a People Manual—it is an intimate love letter written to you from your Father. Through it He invites you daily to experience new and exciting dimensions of His love. The Scriptures are God's Holy Word, delivered by holy men, to teach holy truths, and to make people holy.

It is all well and good to know that the Bible is useful, reliable, and valuable. It is another thing to make it your own in a practical way. It is only profitable if you read it.

Look Inside

How can you make the Word of God more effective in your life as a leader?

Here are five practical ways you can cultivate Habit #3, Knowing and Applying Scripture, into your life—hear, read, study, memorize, meditate. You probably already know these steps, but the question is, *Are you practicing them*? If not, it will take some time for all of them to become a habit.

After reading each of the following explanations of how to bring God's Word alive in your life, take the following steps: evaluate where you are with your own practical application, decide what you plan to do to make it a habit, and set a date and time to begin. Give yourself time to add one discipline to another until all are part of your life. You are in the process of becoming a Lead-Like-Jesus servant leader for life, and it will be better for you to master these one at a time, beginning with the one that most appeals to you. Then you can add another on your own schedule. We are not trying to teach you these skills but rather give you a manual to use in your development.

1. Hear God's Word

Even a child or a person who cannot read can hear the Bible.

> "If anyone has ears to hear, let him hear" (Mark 4:23).

> "Faith comes from hearing the message, and the message is heard through the word of Christ" (Rom. 10:17).

The Parable of the Sower, found in Matt. 13:3–23, lists four kinds of hearers of the Word: (1) the *apathetic* hearer who hears the Word but is not prepared to receive and understand it (v.19); (2) the *superficial* hearer who receives the Word temporarily but does not let it take root in the heart (v.20–21); (3) the *preoccupied* hearer who receives the Word but lets the worries of this world and the desire for other things choke it out (v.22); and (4) the *reproducing* hearer who receives the Word, understands it, bears fruit, and brings forth results (v.23).

- Which kind of hearer are you?

_____

_____

- When it comes to hearing the Word, how effective are you? (1 is poor, 5 is excellent)

| 1 | 2 | 3 | 4 | 5 |

- What are three things you can do this week to be a better hearer of the Word?
  1. _____
  2. _____
  3. _____

2. Read God's Word

> "Blessed is the one who reads the words of this prophecy, and blessed are those who hear it and take to heart what is written in it, because the time is near" (Rev. 1:3).

Here are a few suggestions on how to read the Word so that you hear everything God says to you in your quiet time.

- Allow enough time to read His Word reflectively. God told Joshua, "meditate on it day and night, so that you may be careful to do everything written in it. Then you will be prosperous and successful" (Josh. 1:8).

- Do not try to read so much Scripture at one time that you cannot meditate on its meaning and let God speak directly to you and your situation. Our memory verse for this week is, "But his delight is in the law of the Lord, and on his law he meditates day and night, He is like a tree planted by streams of water, which yields its fruit in season and whose leaf does not wither" (Ps. 1:2–3).

- Balance your reading of the Word. Jesus said, "Everything must be fulfilled that is written about me in the Law of Moses, the Prophets, and the Psalms. Then he opened their minds so they could understand the Scriptures" (Luke 24:44–45).

These three designations of Scripture cover all the counsel of God that will be available to you. You may read the Bible from Genesis to Revelation over a year by reading three chapters a day and five on Sunday. Another plan is to read a chapter from the Old Testament and a chapter from the New Testament each day. Or you might prefer to read through a book of the Bible one chapter a day before moving to another book.

Another valuable practice is to read five Psalms and one Proverb each day. This allows us to work through all of the Psalms and Proverbs in a month. The Psalms are primarily man speaking to God, while the Proverbs are God speaking to man. A thoughtful reading of these each day helps us to use the Psalms to frame our thoughts to God and use the Proverbs to remind us of what God wants for us.

- When it comes to reading the Word, how effective are you? (1 is poor, 5 is excellent)

  1   2   3   4   5

- What are three things you can do this week to be a better reader of the Word?
  1. _____
  2. _____
  3. _____

3. Study God's Word

Revelation 1:3 says: "Blessed is the one who reads the words of this prophesy, and blessed are those who hear it and take to heart what is written in it, because the time is near."

To take it to heart, ask God to show you what His Word means to you and for your life. Jesus promised: "If you obey my commands, you will remain in my love, just as I have obeyed my Father's commands and remain in his love" (John 15:10).

Every time you apply the Word of God to your life, you grow closer to Him. Every time you fail to apply it, you leave the Word, like scattered seed, beside the road where Satan can steal it. Once you have heard His Word, you are prepared to respond to it in prayer and obedience. Jesus said, "If anyone loves me, he will obey my teaching. My Father will love him, and he will come to him and make our home with him" (John 14:23).

When you study the Word you go deeper into it. "The Bereans were of more noble character then the Thessalonians, for they received the message with great eagerness and examined the Scriptures every day to see if what Paul said was true" (Acts 17:11).

- When it comes to studying the Word, how effective are you? (1 is poor, 5 is excellent)

    1   2   3   4   5

- What are three things you can do this week to be a better student of the Word?

    1. _____

    2. _____

    3. _____

4. Memorize God's Word

When you remember the Word, it really lives in you, you live in it, and God's promises become your possessions. "How can a young man keep his way pure? By living according to your word. . . . I have hidden your word in my heart that I might not sin against you" (Ps. 119:9, 11).

Another way you live in the Word and the Word lives in you is to think about it or meditate on it: "His delight is in the law of the Lord, and on his law he meditates day and night" (Ps. 1:2).

Memorization puts God's Word in your head. Meditation puts it in your heart.

- When it comes to memorizing the Word, how effective are you? (1 is poor, 5 is excellent)

    1   2   3   4   5

- What are three things you can do this week to better memorize the Word?

    1. _____

    2. _____

    3. _____

5. Meditate on God's Word

You meditate on God's Word when you concentrate on one verse a week. Select a verse you want to memorize or that has been a key verse in a passage you have just read. Ask the Holy Spirit for His revelation as you meditate. As you memorize a verse (or passage) use the method the Navigators (a group that encourages Bible memorization) recommends—say the name of the book, chapter, and verse(s) fore and aft, as they say. That is, before and after the verse itself. This reinforces the connection between the verse and its location.

- When it comes to meditating on the Word, how effective are you? (1 is poor, 5 is excellent)

           1   2   3   4   5

- What are three things you can do this week to better meditate on the Word?

1. _____

2. _____

3. _____

Look Inside

The psalmist said, "I have hidden your word in my heart that I might not sin against you" (Ps. 119:11). The message of this verse is that allowing God's Word to penetrate your heart can help you resist temptation to sin. On the other hand, you are easy prey for Satan when you are defenseless—and your only defense is the indwelling of God's Word.

- On the line below, place an *X* where you are today based on God's Word being hidden in your heart:

Defenseless-----   -------- ----------------------------------|------------------------------------- -----Defended

- Now place a check mark (✔) where you want to be. What are you going to do about moving from where you are to where you want to be?

_____

_____

_____

_____

_____

Key Concepts

- If you only use the Bible to study and apply its practical wisdom about dealing with people and overcoming internal challenges, it still would stand alone as the greatest book ever written. But the Bible is so much more than a how-to manual for dealing with people; it is an intimate love letter written to you from your Father.

- "All Scripture is God-breathed and is useful for teaching, rebuking, correcting and training in righteousness, so that the man of God may be thoroughly equipped for every good work" (2 Tim. 3:16–17).

- If you haven't stored away the Word of God beforehand, it will be impossible to bring its power into play when you are faced with the hard choices of the day. You can not give what you have not received

- The key ways of glorifying God by taking His word into your life are to:

Hear God's Word

Read God's Word

Study God's

Meditate on God' Word

Memorize God's Word

Apply God's Word

 ## A Point to Ponder

Remember a time you almost made a big mistake and were pulled back from the brink by God's Word. Remember a time the burden was almost too hard to bear and you found comfort in God's Word. Remember a time when the way to go was not clear or it looked too scary and you found courage and confidence in the promises of God. Go now and make new memories with God's Word!

Next Steps

In what area of use and application of God's Word do you feel the most confident?

_____

_____

_____

In which area do you feel the weakest?

_____

_____

_____

What would it take to increase your level of effectiveness in your weaker areas?

_____

_____

_____

THE HABIT OF ACCEPTING GOD'S UNCONDITIONAL LOVE

Quote for Today

God proved His love on the cross. When Christ hung, and bled, and died, it was God saying to the world, "I love you."[3]

Billy Graham

What God's Word Says:

> For God so loved the world that he gave his one and only Son, that whoever believes in him shall not perish but have eternal life. (John 3:16)

The verse above might well be the best-known Bible verse, but what does it really say? The phrase *so loved* often is taken to be a reference to the depth of God's love. However, a further study of the concept produces the paraphrase *loved this way*. Therefore, the verse could be rendered: "God loved the world in this way—He gave His one and only Son so that whoever believes in Him shall not perish but have eternal life."

Pause and Reflect

• God's love for us is revealed in His giving of His Son. How is your love for others revealed?

_____

_____

_____

_____

A Prayer for Today:

Father God, help me acknowledge, accept and rest in your unconditional love for me so that I might unconditionally love those you have called me to lead. In Jesus's Loving Name, Amen!

Today's Topic
THE HABIT OF ACCEPTING GOD'S UNCONDITIONAL LOVE

In seeking to lead like Jesus we will come to points of decision that will reveal where we put our trust and hope. We will continue to face both the fear of negative consequences taking a stand might incur and also the temptation to rely on and worship our own self-accumulated resources and efforts as our sources of self-worth and security.

We live in a world that willfully fuels the fires of pride and fear. We are constantly being lured into believing we can secure a sense of meaning and safety through fads, fashion, and acquiring "more and better" goods.

Standing in absolute contrast to these temporary, always at-risk, never-secure options are the unconditional love and promises of God. It is here and only here that we can find a never-ending supply of what we need to live and lead as Jesus would.

Accepting this reality is often a struggle between acknowledging God's promises as being general in nature and surrendering all your reservations that they are meant for you personally. The power of unconditional love is lived out in your relationships. For example, whenever we ask parents to raise their hands if they love their kids, all hands go up. When we ask parents if they love their kids only if they are successful, all the hands eventually go down. You love your kids unconditionally, right?

If God's love for you were based on your performance to His standards, you would never be free from anxiety. However, if you accept God's unconditional love, you won't be held captive by the world's performance-based philosophies.

• Think about your response to God's unconditional love and mark the one that best matches your thoughts:

_____ I totally accept God's love for me and will live in that reality.

_____ I accept as true God's unconditional love for me, but I still want to earn it.

_____ I can't seem to believe that God unconditionally loves me.

_____ God's unconditional love is incomprehensible to me.

To Lead Like Jesus You Must Love Him

Jesus asked Peter, "Do you love Me?" That question still echoes through the halls of your home and workplace. Your every move is your real response to that question. Like Peter, all of us have given Jesus good reasons to doubt our sincerity. We all fall short!

Read John 21:15–19 and describe how Peter was to prove his love for Jesus.

> When they had finished eating, Jesus said to Simon Peter, "Simon son of John, do you truly love me more than these?" "Yes, Lord," he said, "you know that I love you." Jesus said, "Feed my lambs." Again Jesus said, "Simon son of John, do you truly love me?" He answered, "Yes, Lord, you know that I love you." Jesus said, "Take care of my sheep." The third time he said to him, "Simon son of

John, do you love me?" Peter was hurt because Jesus asked him the third time, "Do you love me?" He said, "Lord, you know all things; you know that I love you." Jesus said, "Feed my sheep. I tell you the truth, when you were younger you dressed yourself and went where you wanted; but when you are old you will stretch out your hands, and someone else will dress you and lead you where you do not want to go." Jesus said this to indicate the kind of death by which Peter would glorify God. Then he said to him, "Follow me!"

Do you love Jesus enough to love His sheep? Jesus didn't ask Peter if he feared Him, respected Him, or admired Him. Jesus wants to see, in the lives of His followers, evidence of their love for Him. Jesus says how you treat other people is how you treat Him. That can be a scary thought!

• Think about your interactions with people within the past twenty-four hours. If how you treated them is a reflection of your love for Jesus, how much do you love Jesus?

_____ slightly more than a root canal

_____ slightly more than rush-hour traffic

_____ a little more than my favorite television show

_____ I'm madly in love with Jesus

To Lead Like Jesus You Must Love Like Jesus

If you do not love Jesus you cannot love the people you lead. Nothing but the love of Christ will compel you to go cheerfully through the difficulties and discouragements you experience as a leader. However, Christ's kind of love will make your work easier, and it will encourage those you lead to serve wholeheartedly.

All individuals need to be heard; they need to be praised; they need to be encouraged; they need to be accepted. As a leader, you need to practice these expressions of love. Why? Because you express your love of Jesus by loving those He puts in your path. Jesus said, "But I tell you who hear me: Love your enemies, do good to those who hate you, bless those who curse you, pray for those who mistreat you" (Luke 6:27–28).

We have discovered that if we let Jesus love others through us and do good things for them, we learn to love them, too.

Look Inside

• What do you want to tell Jesus about His unconditional love?

_____

_____

• What commitment will you make toward loving Him unconditionally?

_____

- How will you let Him love others unconditionally through you?

_____

_____

- How will you allow Jesus to love through you the "unlovable" people in your life?

_____

_____

Key Concepts

- In seeking to lead like Jesus we will come to points of decision that will reveal where we put our trust and hope.
- Standing in absolute contrast to the temporary, always at-risk, never-secure options that possessions, performance and the opinion of others offer are the unconditional love and promises of God. It is here and only here that we can find and be a never-ending supply of what we need to live and lead as Jesus would.
- If you do not love Jesus, you cannot love the people you lead. Nothing but the love of Christ will compel you to go cheerfully through the difficulties and discouragements you experience as a leader.
- All individuals need to be heard; they need to be praised; they need to be encouraged; they need to be accepted. As a leader, you need to practice these expressions of love. Why? Because you express your love of Jesus by loving those He puts in your path.

A Point to Ponder

What price tag do you have a right to put on loving others that hasn't already been paid in full on the Cross?

Next Steps

Write a love letter to God below, expressing your deepest thoughts of love to Him, for Him and about Him.

_____

_____

Now write a love letter to the person with whom you have the most intimate relationship. Are you willing to send it? If not, why not? If yes, send it!

_____

_____

THE HABIT OF MAINTAINING ACCOUNTABILITY RELATIONSHIPS

Quote for Today

Leadership can be a lonely business filled with great amounts of soul-draining human interaction but little soul-filling intimacy. Without some safe-harbor relationships where we can lay down all the armor and weapons needed to face the world and relax in confidence and unguarded communion, we become vulnerable to two debilitating frames of mind and spirit—the victim and the martyr.[4]

Ken Blanchard and Phil Hodges

What God's Word Says

My command is this: Love each other as I have loved you. Greater love has no one than this, that he lay down his life for his friends. You are my friends if you do what I command. I no longer call you servants, because a servant does not know his master's business. Instead I call you friends, for everything that I learned from my Father I have made known to you. (John 15:12–15)

Pause and Reflect

Being a servant leader requires obedience to God. God never abandoned His role as absolute leader, yet He provided a way for us to be His friends. If obedience to God establishes your friendship with Him, how good of a friend to Him are you?

_____

_____

_____

A Prayer for Today

Father God, just as Jesus sought out some close companions to walk with Him, I recognize the need for people in my life with whom I can be open and vulnerable to avoid being blind to my own weaknesses. Help me find truth-telling friends and to be one in return. In Jesus's Name. Amen!

Today's Topic
MAINTAINING ACCOUNTABILITY RELATIONSHIPS

Leadership is lonely business. When we rely on our own perspective of how we are doing, we are bound to slip into convenient rationalizations and blind spots that can quickly undermine our integrity and the trust of those who look to us for leadership.

Henri Nouwen noted a consistent pattern in the daily life of Jesus that proceeded from solitude to community to service. The time Jesus spent in fellowship with His disciples seems to have been for their benefit and His. Among the twelve that He called out to be His apostles, Jesus had a small group of three—Peter, James, and John—with whom He seemed to have a particularly close relationship. He took these three with Him to the Mountain of Transfiguration where He revealed to them, in confidence, the true nature of His being (see Matthew 17:1–9). The same three men were present when He raised the daughter of the synagogue leader from the dead (see Mark 5:21–43). The most poignant and instructive episode involving this inner circle of intimate friendships occurred on the night Jesus was to be arrested and start His final journey to the Cross.

In Matthew 26:37–38, we read: "He took Peter and the two sons of Zebedee along with him, and he began to be sorrowful and troubled. Then He said to them, 'My soul is overwhelmed with sorrow to the point of death. Stay here and keep watch with me.'"

Leadership can be a lonely business filled with great amounts of soul-draining human interaction but little soul-filling intimacy. Without some safe-harbor relationships in which we can lay down all the armor and weapons needed to face the world and relax in confidence and unguarded communion, we become vulnerable to two debilitating frames of mind—the victim and the martyr. Allowed to blossom into resentment or self-justification, these twin demons have been the downfall of many a leader in every walk of life.

Jesus emphasized the importance of a sense of community in His prayer for His followers to attain the joy that He had in unity and fellowship with His Father. Jesus told His disciples,

> As the Father has loved me, so have I loved you. Now remain in my love....
> My command is this: Love each other as I have loved you. Greater love has no
> one than this, that he lay down his life for his friends. You are my friends if you
> do what I command. I no longer call you servants, because a servant does not
> know his master's business. Instead, I have called you friends, for everything
> that I learned from my Father I have made known to you. (John 15:9, 12–15)

When we rely on our own perspective of how we are doing, we are bound to slip into convenient rationalizations and blind spots that can quickly undermine our integrity and the trust of those who look to us for leadership.

Truth-Tellers

We all need trusted truth-tellers, preferably those not directly impacted by what we do, who can help keep us on course. If you can't name any active truth-tellers in your life, or if you have avoided or undervalued the ones you have, it's time to change. Having truth-tellers is probably the greatest resource for growth that you can have.

Bring truth-tellers into your life, and they will speak to you honestly if they know you'll listen. It doesn't mean you have to do everything that they say, but they want to be heard.

Being open to feedback from other people is not the only way to grow. Being willing to disclose vulnerabilities to other people is another. We're all vulnerable. We all fall short. Don't be afraid to share your vulnerability.

 ## Look Inside

If you can't name any active truth-tellers in your life, or if you have avoided or undervalued the ones you have, it's time to change.

* Name the people in your life that you rely on to tell you what you need to hear even if it hurts:

  _____

  _____

  _____

  _____

  _____

* List three things that you do to make it easy for your truth-tellers help you stay on track:
  1. _____
  2. _____
  3. _____

* List three things you do that make it difficult for your truth-tellers to help you stay on track:
  1. _____
  2. _____
  3. _____

* Name the people in your life that are relying on you as their truth teller.
  1. _____
  2. _____
  3. _____

- How would you rate yourself as a truth-teller for the people you just named?

Person # 1

_____ Well intentioned but inactive

_____ Occasionally helpful when not busy with other things

_____ Always available to listen, offering advice only when asked and willing to tell the truth in love

Person # 2

_____ Well intentioned but inactive

_____ Occasionally helpful when not busy with other things

_____ Always available to listen, offering advice only when asked and willing to tell the truth in love

Person # 3

_____ Well intentioned but inactive

_____ Occasionally helpful when not busy with other things

_____ Always available to listen, offering advice only when asked and willing to tell the truth in love

Key Concepts

- Leadership can be a lonely business filled with great amounts of soul-draining human interaction but little soul-filling intimacy. Without some safe-harbor relationships, we become vulnerable to two debilitating frames of mind—the victim and the martyr.
- Truth-tellers protect us from ourselves by being always ready to listen, giving advice when asked, and being trusted to love us anyway, warts and all.

A Point to Ponder

What happens to leaders left in isolation? Has God put someone in your path that needs your help, acceptance and encouragement?

_____

_____

_____

_____

Next Steps

Identify one person you trust and ask them to join you as a truth teller about your effectiveness and style of leadership.

Invite three others and form a supportive relationship group based on the Lead Like Jesus model.

appendix

The Prayer of a Novice

Father, thank You for this chance to learn something new! As I seek to honor You by submitting to the instructions of my teacher, help me to approach the learning process with a teachable spirit. Help me to be patient with myself and with my teacher. Give me the courage to be willing to ask questions when things are not clear and not to be afraid to look a little foolish when trying things for the first time. Lord Jesus, help me to keep my pride in check so I can learn what I don't know. As You were obedient when under instruction, help me to be obedient so that I may grow in wisdom and in my ability to serve You by serving others. In Jesus's name, Amen!

Second Novice Prayer

Father, You know that this opportunity is something I am not looking forward to or excited about, yet here it is. Lord, help me see it as an opportunity to grow in endurance and grace and to be a witness of the strength that comes from You.

Lord Jesus, help me find new meaning in what I am assigned to do. Just as You learned and labored in this world at a common trade, help me remember to do all things for the glory of God. Speak to my heart, put a new song in my mouth, but most of all, Father, teach me to trust You in the midst of this raging storm. I know that You will go before me, and in the dark night You will carry me. In You I put my trust. In Jesus's strong name, Amen!

The Prayer of an Apprentice

Lord, I am learning a new task, and it's turning out to be harder than I thought! By now, I expected to know more about it than I do and to be able to perform on my own more than I can. Lord, I don't want to fail, and I don't want to seem stupid or silly for asking questions to which I ought to know the answers. Help me accept the fact that everything may not come easily and that I have to be accountable for having a teachable attitude, even when the going gets rough. Help me focus my thoughts, and take my anxiety from me. Teach me how to do this task in the right way with a patient and forgiving heart and to quickly apply the new learning so that I don't forget. In Jesus's name, Amen!

Second Apprentice Prayer

Lord, this task seems harder than I thought it was. Maybe I'm not cut out to do it, but I know that You have faithfully brought me to this place and that You believe in me. Help me to believe in myself, too! I want to do this assignment with the right heart and mind and to learn as much as I can, so remove my fears and false pride so that while learning, I can serve as well. I want to demonstrate You to those around me, so calm my mind and help me do this well. In Jesus's name, Amen!

The Prayer of a Journeyman

Father, thank you for putting the teachers and experiences in my path that have brought me to this season of skill where I am able to produce high-quality results from my personal efforts. Lord, thank you for allowing me to be excited about where my work fits in and that it has meaning. Because I have been at it a while, sometimes my enthusiasm and excitement decline, and I get down on myself and others. Lord, help renew a right spirit in me. Help me regain a sense of purpose and stewardship of the gifts, talent, and opportunities You gave me. Help me be an encouragement to those who are in the learning process and to be a good model and witness for you. In Jesus's name, Amen.

Second Journeyman Prayer

Lord, I don't know where to go from here. Because of some setbacks and mistakes I take responsibility for, I have lost some of my self-confidence and inspiration. I feel reluctant to step out of my comfort zone to teach others what I know or to act in a leadership position. Lord, I know You have placed me here to be a light on a hill. Help me listen to wise counsel, be totally honest about my current situation, and be open to taking a positive step back to the level of service and commitment I once enjoyed under Your wings of mercy and grace. In Jesus's name, Amen.

The Prayer of Master/Teacher

Lord, You have blessed me with the ability and opportunity to develop into a master of this role or task You put before me. You have walked with me through the growing process and have allowed me to remain humble enough and teachable enough to become an expert. Help me now, Lord, to take what I have been given and use it to serve others by example and by sharing my knowledge. Lord, keep me ever mindful of the debt I owe to You and to those who taught me so well. Give me patience to faithfully and carefully teach those I serve and to avoid the temptation to become arrogant or complacent in my expertise. In Jesus's name, Amen.

Second Master/Teacher Prayer

Lord, You know that I get tired and weary of teaching, leading, and serving those new to these tasks. I need Your strength, character, and perseverance to do this again. Help me see the reward in doing this, because it is You that I serve. Let me nurture the enthusiasm of the novices and calm the fear of the apprentices. Give me patience to respond with excitement to their questions and concerns. Help me to not reflect an unhappy heart but a heart that is full of love and compassion for each one of them and their situation. Let the title of "master/teacher" remind me of my own Master and Teacher—the Lord Jesus! In His name, Amen.

The Prayer of an Instructor of Novices

Father, today I greet a group of novices. For the most part, they are excited about their new assignment and eager to learn. Some already know something about their tasks, some know nothing, and some think they know things but they are the wrong things. As I face them, Father, give me the grace to love each one as You would. Help me remember what it was like for me when I was just starting out and to be sensitive to both their fears and lack of understanding of what is involved in learning this new task or role. Give me the wisdom to know what they need to know and clear thoughts as I consider each task to be taught. Help my presentation to be meaningful to each one, so that learning will take place. Allow my face to reflect You rather than what I may feel about each question that is asked. Most of all, may they see in me a reflection of You. In Jesus's name, Amen.

The Prayer of a Mentor of Apprentices

Father, today I will continue to guide the learning path of those I have committed to train. So far, they have progressed from unskilled novices to partially trained apprentices. Most of them have found the new work more difficult than anticipated. Some have voiced frustration and discouragement with themselves, with me, and with the whole learning process. Some, on the other hand, are overconfident and impatient to move on before they are really well-prepared. Lord, I will need patience and wisdom as I greet them today. Help me to remain sensitive to their individual needs. Some will need encouragement. Help me to see and praise their progress. Some will need to have their inflated pride in their initial accomplishments tempered with a sense of what they still need to learn. Help me to be patient but firm. May I faithfully teach the new tasks with skill, integrity, and wisdom and avoid delegating work prematurely. Thanks, Father, for this opportunity to grow and develop in my own experiences as well as to teach others. I know that in this I am following the way of Jesus. In His name, Amen.

The Prayer of an Inspirer of Journeymen

Father, today I am called to serve the needs of journeymen. These people know how to do a good job and have proven to be reliable individual performers. What I may be called on to provide is help so that they may reconnect with greater meaning and purpose or encouragement so that they may perform it in a new environment. Maybe it will be to provide reassurance to someone who has suffered a setback that has made him question his own abilities. Father, help me to be slow to speak, slow to offer advice or prescribe ready-made solutions. Help me to be patient and understanding. Guide my thoughts and actions so that the people I am seeking to help will be encouraged to draw on what they know and have experienced and may be able to make positive choices for their future. In Jesus's name, Amen.

The Prayer of a Commissioner of Master/Teachers

Lord, what an awesome time! The people I have guided through the learning process have arrived at the point of being fully inspired and equipped not only to do the work on their own but also to serve and teach others. They have been entrusted to me for a little while, and I have faithfully imparted my knowledge to them, and in that we both have grown. I have learned as much from them as they have learned from me. Father, help me send them from this learning experience with a sense of my confidence in them and my appreciation for their teachable spirits. As You sent out Your apostles to spread the good news and assured them of Your constant availability, help me send my students with the same assurances. Lord, part of me doesn't want to let them go. I know some will experience difficulties and some will reap rewards. Some will have to work harder than others, while some will have an easy time. Each is a unique individual created in Your image. Bless each one. In Jesus's name, Amen.

notes

Introduction

1. Inspired by the *Commentaries on the Whole Bible* by Matthew Henry

Week 1

1. Lead Like Jesus, pg. 13
2. Ibid, 18.
3. Ibid, 19.
4. Ibid, 25.
5. Greene, Graham. *The Ministry of Fear*
6. Lead Like Jesus, 26
7. Ibid, 27.

Week 2

1. Kelly, Bob, *Worth Repeating* (Grand Rapids: Kregel, 2003), 311.
2. Ibid, 97.
3. Lead Like Jesus, pg. 51
4. Kelly, Bob, *Worth Repeating* (Grand Rapids: Kregel, 2003), 120.
5. Ibid, 62
6. Blanchard, Ken and Norman Vincent Peale, *The Power of Ethical Management*
7. Smith, Fred, *You and Your Network*

Week 3

1. Lead Like Jesus, pg. 85
2. Winifred Newman
3. Ken Blanchard and Jesse Stoner, *Full Steam Ahead: The Power of Visioning* (San Francisco: Barrett-Koehler, 2003).

4. Richard Nelson Bolles, *What Color Is Your Parachute?* (Berkeley, CA: Ten Speed Press, 1983)

5. Laurie Beth Jones, *The Path: Creating Your Own Mission Statement for Work and Life.* (New York: Hyperion Press, 1996), p. 3.

6. Kelly, Bob, *Worth Repeating* (Grand Rapids: Kregel, 2003), 356.

Week 4

1. Lead Like Jesus, p. 121

2. Kelly, Bob, *Worth Repeating* (Grand Rapids: Kregel, 2003), 37.

3. Ibid, 210.

4. Ibid, 123.

5. Ibid, 334.

Week 5

1. Henry and Richard Blackaby, *Spiritual Leadership* (Nashville: Broadman and Holman, 2001).

2. Lead Like Jesus, pg. 145.

3. Ibid, 149

4. Ibid, 77.

Week 6

1. Kelly, Bob, *Worth Repeating* (Grand Rapids: Kregel, 2003), 276.

2. Ibid, 28.

3. Ibid, 144.

4. Lead Like Jesus, 180.

Ken Blanchard

Few have impacted the day-today management of people and companies more than Ken Blanchard As a prominent author with over three dozen books including *The One Minute Manager*, speaker and business consultant, Ken is universally characterized as one of the most insightful, powerful and compassionate men in business today. Speaking from the heart with warmth and humor, he is a polished storyteller who makes the seemingly complex easy to understand.

With a personal faith in Jesus Christ, Ken recognizes and lifts up Jesus as the greatest leadership role model of all time. He co-founded The Center for Faithwalk Leadership, now known as Lead Like Jesus, in 1999 with a mission "to inspire and equip people to lead like Jesus."

Ken, his wife, Margie, two adult children and three grand-children live in Southern California. He is the co-founder, with his wife, Margie, and Chief Spiritual Officer of the Ken Blanchard Companies. With a Ph.D. from Cornell University, he has been a college professor, an imaginative entrepreneur, and a much sought after business guru. He is an avid golfer and a friend to many!

Phil Hodges

Phil Hodges currently serves as director of product development at the Center for Faithwalk Leadership (now known as Lead Like Jesus), which he and Ken Blanchard co-founded in 1999. Lead Like Jesus is a nonprofit organization dedicated to inspiring and equipping people to lead like Jesus.

In 1997, Phil concluded a thirty-five year career with Xerox Corporation and U.S. Steel to serve as a Consulting Partner with The Ken Blanchard Companies before co-founding Lead Like Jesus.

In addition to helping leaders of faith walk their talk in the marketplace, Phil developed a passion for bringing effective leadership principles into the church during six years as Chairman of the Elder Council in his local congregation. He is a co-author of three books: *Leadership by the Book* with Ken Blanchard and Bill Hybels, and *The Servant Leader* and *Lead Like Jesus: Lessons from the Greatest Leadership Role Model of All Time* both with Ken Blanchard.

Phil and his wife, Jane Kinnaird Hodges, live in Southern California where they are involved daily in their happiest season of influence as parents and grandparents in their expanding family.

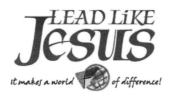

3506 Professional Circle • Augusta, GA 30907
800.383.6890
LeadLikeJesus.com

We have all seen leaders, in corporate America, exploit privileges of position bringing ruin to employees and investors. Meanwhile citizens of under-developed countries languish in poverty and hopelessness in a leadership vacuum. At the same time all across the country, the witness and ministry of churches are compromised and stymied by a crisis of integrity in their leaders. In stark contrast to the failures and foibles of 21st Century leadership stands the perfect leadership role model – Jesus of Nazareth.

Lead Like Jesus, co-founded in 1999, by Ken Blanchard, co-author of *The One Minute Manager*, and his longtime friend, Phil Hodges imagines a world in which leaders serve rather than rule, a world in which they give rather than take. We imagine leaders who seek to produce results from service and sacrifice rather than from power and position. We recognize this only happens as leaders adopt Jesus as their leadership role model and grow in His likeness.

We exist to help leaders of all shapes, sizes, ages and aspirations to explore and express the leadership principles Jesus lived. To that end we are both humbled and honored to be entrusted with the stewardship of this vision - 6.8B souls served daily by the impact of people leading like Jesus.

In Matthew 20, Jesus expressed His view of leadership in His *Not So With You* mandate. This principle is a driving force of Lead Like Jesus.

Our work is centered around three defining distinctives:

Distinctive # 1 - A New Definition of Leadership
Anytime you seek to influence the thinking, behavior or development of people in their personal or professional lives, you are taking on the role of a leader

Distinctive # 2 - A Defined Framework
HEART – Intentions and motivations of a leader

HEAD – beliefs about leadership and influence

HANDS – methods and behaviors of a leader

HABITS – daily disciplines to keep a leader focused

Distinctive # 3 - A Perfect Model
JESUS

To express the equipping mandate, Lead Like Jesus offers a variety of opportunities for leaders to deepen their commitment to more clearly model the leadership of Jesus. Visit LeadLikeJesus.com for up-to-date information on these and other opportunities. These may include:

LARGE, ONE DAY SIMULCAST EVENTS... with a stellar cast of speakers who express how Jesus has transformed their lives and leadership.

LEADERSHIP ENCOUNTER FACILITATOR TRAINING... A workshop designed to provide the training, resources and discussions to enable a person to lead the two day Leadership Encounter in their spheres of influence. Facilitator Care, ongoing training and other resources are provided as part of facilitator training.

RESOURCES...Lead Like Jesus provides a variety of tools to equip people in the marketplace, the church and the home to lead like Jesus everywhere. Use them for personal enjoyment, training or teaching others.

WORKPLACE MINISTRY...An ideal opportunity for expressing the Lead Like Jesus concepts in a workplace setting. Lead Like Jesus offers resources to enhance workplace ministries using DVDs and teaching guides.

COACHING...Recognizing that learning is enhanced when coupled with coaching, Lead Like Jesus is developing a cadre of coaches around the Lead Like Jesus concepts.

DESKTOP DEVOTIONS...Lead Like Jesus reminders delivered to your in box three times a week. Visit LeadLikeJesus.com to sign up for these free devotions.

SPEAKERS BUREAU...Bring Lead Like Jesus to your community. Choose from a variety of well-known speakers. Call 800.383.6890 or visit LeadLikeJesus.com.

> **!!!! FACILITATOR GUIDE FOR GROUP STUDY !!!!**
> Visit LeadLikeJesus.com and enter the online store. Add the FREE Facilitator Guide to your cart and use code SG2007. The free download will be available to you immediately upon checkout.